4/13/95

Alicia,

    Many happy years of gardening!

      Love,

        Daddy & Adelle

GARDENING IN THE SOUTH

with

Don Hastings

VEGETABLES & FRUITS

GARDENING IN THE SOUTH

with
Don Hastings

VEGETABLES & FRUITS

All illustrations property of Taylor Publishing
Company; new illustrations created for this work by
Anne Irene Hurley.

Photographs by the author with the exception of a few
graciously supplied by his father.

Designed by Bonnie Baumann

Copyright 1988 by Donald M. Hastings, Jr.

Published by Taylor Publishing Company
        1550 West Mockingbird Lane
        Dallas, Texas 75235

Library of Congress Cataloging in Publication Data

Hastings, Don.
   Vegetables and fruits / [new illustrations by Anne
   Irene Hurley].
   p. cm.—(Gardening in the South with Don
   Hastings)
   Includes index.
   1. Vegetable gardening—Southern States. 2. Fruit-
culture—Southern States. I. Title. II. Series: Hastings,
Don. Gardening in the South with Don Hastings.
SB321.5.H37 1988   635'.0975—dc19   88-10181 CIP
ISBN 0-87833-599-4

Printed in the United States of America

10 9 8 7 6 5 4 3 2

In Loving Memory of My Mother
Louise B. Hastings
1901–1987

A noted horticulturist and flower artist whose inspiration pushed me ever higher in our beloved field.

And To

The wonderful people of Barangay Nazareth in the central Philippines who so warmly accepted me as we shared the great adventure of introducing high technology vegetable production to that tropical country.

Acknowledgments

The preparation and writing of the three volumes of this series could never have been done without the help and support of my wonderful family. Our gardening has always been a unified effort. Thus Betsy, Don III, and Chris are as much a part of these books as I. In addition, Betsy has read every word and applied her fabulous love and understanding of the English language to my efforts at setting down on paper what I have learned about growing things over the years. My name may be on the title page but the author is really the family as a whole, for without it these books would never have been.

In Volume 1 of *Gardening in the South*, I listed a great number of people who have been so much help and inspiration throughout my horticultural life.

In that list were several who have been particularly helpful in my efforts at mastering vegetable and fruit production. These are: My father, Donald M. Hastings, Sr., whose knowledge and insight into vegetables for the southern United States inspired me in my interest and love for vegetable gardening; Hubert Nicholson who gave me so much help in developing my interest and knowledge about fruits; John Huyck who shared so much of his vegetable production genius; Bernardino Ballesteros who spent so many days with me deciphering all the insects and diseases which plagued our vegetables in the tropics; and Paul Johnson whose neighborly help here in Sweet Apple meant so much to me.

In addition to the above are a number of people who have been particularly helpful in fruit and vegetable horticulture.

W. Ray Hastings, my uncle, was one of the originators of the All-American Selections for determining the best new garden seed varieties and generously shared his vibrant ideas with me.

Melchor A. Tan, a fabulous farmer in the Philippines, helped translate my high-tech approach into practical techniques.

Aubrey Owens, one of the most knowledgeable people, ever, in the field of Southern muscadines and scuppernongs, provided much valuable assistance.

Ireneo Galve III, my young friend Bong-Bong, quickly learned to use my camera and climbed to the top of coconut trees where he so capably took pictures of the vegetable trial project and most of the pictures of me at work there.

CONTENTS

INTRODUCTION

This second volume of *Gardening in the South* will be about growing food in your garden and I must begin by telling you frankly that this is my favorite part of the gardening adventure. I do like growing things which can be harvested and brought to the table. I am sure that my family will never starve if I stop this part of my gardening experience, nor do we reduce our food budget by all that much. It still is the best part of gardening to me.

There is, in me, a great need for making a part of my garden productive. Over and over all kinds of people tell me this feeling is something that is important. One of my fondest memories is of conducting a class on vegetable gardening in which there was a housewife, a waitress, a large corporation president, and an ex-president of a university, among many others. To this diverse group came an understanding and mutuality which I have seldom seen. It resulted in everyone having a great deal of fun as the five-session class progressed and the techniques of growing vegetables from seed to harvest were learned. It was one of the few times when my discussions of soil preparation were as enthusiastically listened to as my discussions on seeding and harvesting. As my boys say, they were really into it!

Fruits and vegetables have been an integral part of man's gardening experience through much of recorded history. Tombs of the Pharaohs were painted with murals depicting many vegetables which came by the caravan routes from the Orient. In Europe, early discoveries of unknown fruits and vegetables by famous explorers were carefully brought by ship

An Egyptian tomb mural showing daily life

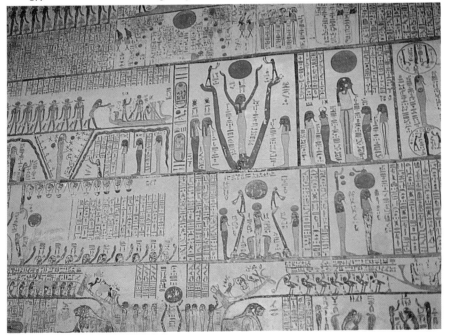

Desert children whose diet is beans and bread

from as far away as the Pacific. Conquerors took with them their favorites and introduced them to the subjugated populations. In the vegetable descriptions, I have traced some of these interesting origins, not just for background information, but to show the lengths that our forebears went to bring their favorites to this country. Early settlers brought with them many native fruits and vegetables from their homelands. To this day the descendants of the original Salzburgers, who settled near the coast of Georgia, keep alive many interesting and useful strains from the old days.

Vegetables and fruits are not always in the diet of many people of this earth. Compared to the cost of grain crops and dried beans, vegetables and fruits cost much more than the preponderance of people can afford. The price of one tomato in the market exceeds the price of many people's daily ration of rice, dried beans, or wheat. Unless they can grow their own fruits and vegetables, most people must do without.

There are always detractors who cite spurious statistics that each tomato a vegetable gardener grows will cost two or three times as much as one from the market. How they miss the point! We Americans have the best agricultural technology on earth and commercially produce the best fresh vegetables in the field. However, our harvest costs are so high that wherever possible they are machine gathered. This necessitates harvesting before the proper maturity and thus before the best quality level is reached. Tomatoes must be harvested while still immature to withstand the rough treatment of the machine picker. Then they are treated with ethylene gas to turn them red so that you will buy them—who would buy a green-colored tomato? Now they are nice and red in color, but still immature. No wonder they taste like nothing at all. The European consumers refuse to fall for this trick and as a result they have much higher quality tomatoes in their markets.

Machine harvesting generally breaks the ends off snapbeans which causes greater dehydration and loss of quality. You never see a machine-harvested bean on the market in Europe or the Orient. They get theirs all lined up with the stem still attached. There is no loss of quality from broken ends in their markets.

The high cost of production has also driven our vegetable farms far from the major markets. Time causes deterioration of quality in fresh vegetables. It has been stated that sweet corn loses almost fifty percent of its

EAACO's tomatoes were all harvested by hand.

EAACO's tomatoes are packed naturally red.

EAACO's harvesters

sugar in the first twenty-four hours after picking. The long time between commercial fields and our tables tremendously reduces quality.

To get the best quality fresh vegetables to eat, we must grow them in our own gardens. That is what this part of our gardening adventure will help you do.

There is such excitement producing fresh vegetables and fruits from my own plantings, and for me, it is the greatest joy in gardening. Like most gardeners, I love to cut a bouquet of roses, pick a camellia from my Lady Clare bush, look out the window at our annual bed, or cut a sprig of quince to force during the cold winter; in fact, growing any kind of plant and seeing the results is a thrill to me. But growing things for use on our table is the best part of gardening for me. There is something exhilarating about producing food on your own land. To me it is the essence of growing things.

Although my vocation deals with growing things, over the years the produce from my individual gardening efforts on my own land has given me the greatest sense of accomplishment. When Don and Chris were very young, we grew a bed of sweet potatoes each year. At harvest time Betsy and I would be as excited as they were when they dove into a clump of soil and removed a beautiful big sweet potato. To all of us it was like a huge gold nugget.

No gathering of friends at our home in Sweet Apple is complete without a walk through the vegetable garden. Our memories abound of friends who have shared our harvests or have eaten Silver Queen raw off the stalk for the first time. They can't believe what they taste. Sharing the harvest is a cherished part of our life. A basket of fresh tomatoes, zucchini, or sweet corn given away is one of the best aspects of friendship. Our Christmas giving always includes gifts from our garden. A jar of my grape jelly, a bottle of pepper sauce, or Betsy's specialty, pepper jelly, seem to be the most welcomed gifts from us.

Egyptian desert children with pita bread for lunch

Joemarie Galve, a Filipino worker, in his first crop of Silver Queen sweet corn

Life is more fulfilling when we are productive. I am always happiest when I am working on a project which involves growing fresh fruit or produce. I have produced vegetables in former desert land in Egypt and on a beautiful, tranquil tropical island in the Philippines. No matter where I introduce the concept of growing fresh food, the excitement is the same.

In Egypt, many of our workers who lived their lives in the desert on a basic diet of foule beans and pita bread had never known fresh tomatoes or muskmelons, much less broccoli, true sweet corn, or lettuce. When the harvest started, they ate almost as much as they picked. You should have seen how the teenagers' growth increased!

In the Philippines where fresh fruits and vegetables are common, the excitement of a new crop ready for harvest was still as great. From our people's own efforts, new types of vegetables were being harvested and eaten for perhaps the first time.

A successful harvest, after one has triumphed over insects, diseases, growth problems, and weather disasters, is the greatest reward a grower of plants can have.

In the present volume, I will take you into this world of gardening which many people unfortunately never see. You will see vegetables which you may never have grown or even eaten. You will see where many of our common vegetables came from. We will talk about fruiting plants and fruit trees which are wonderful adjuncts to the home landscape.

Many of you have grown vegetables before. Your way may be different from mine. Your favorite variety may not be mine. Perhaps you like rhubarb; I don't. Differences of opinion help all of us garden better. Never abandon a tried and proven practice simply because I have a different one. First try any new, reasonable idea, type of vegetable, or variety in a limited way. See how it stacks up against your tried and true ones. Then accept it if it is better.

The first volume of this series, *Trees, Shrubs, and Lawns*, covered the basics of gardening in the South such as soils, climate, and basic planting. I hope that it has been of great help to you. In that volume I gave you some of my thoughts on how to approach gardening in our part of the world. I quote the following statement from that volume because I believe it with all my heart: "Perhaps, most of all, we will learn to have fun while gardening. Gardening with a vengeance is all right if there is a big smile on your face. But deliver me from a dour, sad-faced, grumpy gardener. It is impudence to God and nature to be grumpy in a garden. Either growing things must be a happy time, or in these days of so much activity it will never be done. Even if the tiller won't start or the fertilizer is lumpy, still, kick a clod in frustration and then smile. The garden is a place to be happy while you're being productive."

NAMES OF VEGETABLES AND FRUITS

In the first volume of this series, *Trees, Shrubs, and Lawns*, I used the new term "cultivar" for what we have traditionally called "variety." This is the currently-accepted method of naming a horticultural variant which is different in a horticultural sense but not in a taxonomic or botanical sense.

In the world of trees, shrubs, flowers, fruits, and even grasses, this new system works well. However, you will seldom, if ever, find the term used with vegetables. Silver Queen is still called a variety of sweet corn; Monte Carlo is a variety of tomato.

Therefore you will find the use of the term "variety" rather than "cultivar" throughout the discussion of vegetables. Even though the term "cultivar" is correct, I have continued using the old term "variety" to make it easier for you to get what you want from your seed supplier.

GARDENING IN THE SOUTH
with
Don Hastings
VEGETABLES & FRUITS

CHAPTER 1

GROWING YOUR OWN GROCERIES

Now more than ever before in history, people are eating more fresh, non-processed vegetables. Salad bars are a popular addition to restaurant fare. Raw vegetables are seen presented in a variety of ways. Nutritionists and medical experts recommend raw vegetables as a useful addition to the diet.

I have seen this trend increase the demand for high-quality vegetables in the market and have gone to such places as Egypt and the Philippines to grow them so that the supply will be continuous throughout the year. I grow vegetables in my own garden because home-grown, freshly-picked vegetables are of higher quality and taste better than when picked less than fully ripe.

Vegetable growing is almost universal. There are few places in the world where some type of vegetable will not grow. In our area, we are fortunate that there is a wide range of vegetable types suited to our soils and climate.

Vegetable growing is rewarding because of the wonderful sense of productivity it gives to the gardener. It is also fun! Even on our commercial farms, there seems to be more happiness in a harvest of tomatoes or lettuce or corn than in one of rice or wheat. No matter how large or small your crop, the first ripe fruit blesses the faith you had when the tiny seed was planted.

The author's desert vegetable project in West Nobaria, Egypt.

The author's pilot test project in the Philippines.

To many of us native Southerners, the term "garden" refers strictly to the vegetable garden. Not long ago a garden catalog listed only home garden vegetables and supplies. When Extension Service bulletins referred to garden plots, they meant vegetables. Momma's flower beds and borders were another matter entirely.

Today, though gardening encompasses many other facets of growing things, many of us still think of the vegetable garden as "the garden" in its best sense.

The Englishman grows his annuals, perennials, and roses; the Southerner grows his tomatoes, peppers, squash, beans, and corn. It is our desire and heritage to grow vegetables.

Many of the South's new gardeners are following in this tradition. They too have succumbed to the immense satisfaction and feeling of productivity found in bringing a mess of beans, a sack of tomatoes, or an armful of corn from the garden to the kitchen.

Freshly picked vegetables *are better*. They bear little resemblance to store bought" produce. Listen to the songs of praise for the home-grown tomato. Listen to the experts with their statistics on sugar loss from sweet

A Southern vegetable garden is a blessing to any home.

Fresh garden Zucchini is better than that from a store.

Fresh tomatoes bear little resemblence to U.S. market tomatoes.

corn in the first twenty-four hours after harvest. No wonder store-bought corn never tastes like the field corn we ate when I was a child. There is something very different about the taste of fresh vegetables from the garden.

CHOOSING THE LOCATION

A vegetable garden can be any size which suits your way of living. One of the most productive gardens I have ever seen belonged to a friend with a garden spot smaller than many living rooms. Apartment and condo-minium dwellers can grow vegetables in tubs, planters, and pots, while we country folk work our quarter-acre and half-acre plots. We are all still vegetable gardeners.

A postage-stamp size vegetable garden can still produce well.

An apartment dweller can have a few fresh tomatoes from a hanging basket.

A ruggedly individualistic "front yard" vegetable planting

The author's vegetable garden meets the criteria for the optimum garden location.

Gone are the days, for most of us, when the vegetable garden could be carved out of a cornfield near the house. There are all sorts of strict rules for the location of a vegetable garden, but today most of us have to be pragmatic and use the best solutions possible on our lot. Space and land usage must fit into the whole landscape plan. Only the most ruggedly individualistic gardener will place his vegetable plot beside the front walk because that is the perfect location.

The criteria for growing vegetables cannot be ignored. But when your spot doesn't fit the criteria perfectly, there are usually ways to compromise. So let's look at the list of criteria for selecting a vegetable garden site:

- six hours full sun per day
- good drainage
- relatively level ground
- rich loamy soil
- rows running north and south
- few trees near garden

SIX HOURS FULL SUN PER DAY

Full sun is absolutely the most necessary ingredient for a successful location. Vegetables *must* have sunshine to produce well. If you start with a summer garden, choose the site where the sun shines fully *at least* six hours each day during the time from the spring equinox until the fall equinox. Perhaps you have enough sunshine only in the fall and winter when the trees are bare. If this is the case, then consider placing most of your emphasis on cool season crops. It is quite possible to have your summer garden in one location and your spring, fall, and winter gardens in another. If you have less than six hours full sun, try a few different types of greens and perhaps leaf lettuce since these take less sun than other vegetables. If you don't have at least six hours sunshine anywhere on your property, you'd better not try growing any vegetables but the leafy ones.

GOOD DRAINAGE

The second basic need for growing vegetables is soil that drains well. Remember that vegetables grow poorly with wet feet. Look for a garden site where the soil is not consistently damp and sticky. Beware of low areas where water tends to stand. Algae and moss are sure signs of poor drainage. Sub-surface drainage is as important as surface drainage.

When inspecting your landscape for the site, dig a spadeful of soil from each prospective spot. Feel the soil and smell it. If it feels sticky and smells sour, it's poor soil and you should look for another location.

Correcting Poor Drainage

Poor drainage can be corrected if there are no other available locations, but it takes some work. Sometimes just working the soil deeply and adding large amounts of humus will correct poor drainage, especially if surface

Poor drainage is one of vegetables' worst enemies.

Poor drainage killed this row of beans.

drainage is the primary problem. In especially bad locations, you can install drain tile, using common land tile or septic tank field line. For either, you need to dig deep trenches and lay the line in the bottom on a slight decline, toward an area such as a ditch or stream where the subsurface water can be carried away. For small gardens, a popular method of correcting poor drainage is to use raised beds, building them with railroad crossties or some other heavy, treated lumber. Remember, however, to keep the entire root zone of the plants above the original surface of the soil. Remember also to use soil which has been prepared well and has good drainage qualities to fill these raised beds.

RELATIVELY LEVEL GROUND

Here we must compromise. If the ground is too flat, the soil is often poorly drained. If the ground is too steep, it is hard to work and may wash severely. Level land is easier to lay out, plow, and cultivate. If you try to plow on a slope, the tiller will "ride" downhill making it very difficult to use even on a slight slope. If you allow your rows to go down the slope (like the tiller wants to go), severe washing will occur when it rains. When the garden site is not level, run the rows across the slope to prevent washing.

RICH LOAMY SOIL

You may be surprised to find fertility so far down the criteria list. It is perhaps the easiest of all faults to correct. To begin with, almost all of the soils in the southeastern United States have been badly depleted through years of misuse. The innate richness of the soil which the early settlers found has been ruined by years of neglect, and cotton farming, and now, bulldozers. All of our soil must be improved in order to grow any plants well, especially vegetables, by adding humus and nutrients on a regular basis. You must follow the rules set forth in the first volume of these books on preparing the soil if you want to have a successful vegetable garden.

NORTH-SOUTH ROWS

What earthly difference does it make which way your rows run? A lot! The right direction for rows is running north and south. Think about the logic. Since the sun will cross over the rows evenly as it moves east to west, both sides of the plant will receive the same amount of sunlight. Also, in our part of the world, the sun is almost always in the Southern meridian, even in the summer. Therefore, if you were to run the rows east and west, the

The author's vegetable planting area is now rich and friable after many years of improvement. It was once cotton land.

Cotton farming depleted our soils.

Crimson Clover used as a winter crop to improve the soil.

south side of the row would always receive more sun than the north side. For winter crops, when the sun is in the southern sky, some vegetable growers run rows east and west and plant on the south side of a raised bed to gather warmth for earlier and better growth. But for the rest of the year, it is best to stick to north and south rows.

This is an ideal theory and should be followed only when all other criteria can accommodate such a scheme. Never run rows up and down an incline just to have north-south rows. The problems created by washing will far exceed the advantages of that extra sunlight.

FEW TREES NEAR THE GARDEN

Be sure that you have not chosen a vegetable garden site near any large trees. Placing your garden too near trees creates several problems for vegetables. One is that you will have too much shade. Another is tree root competition, which can stunt plants badly. Often areas which get good sunlight but are still in the root zone of a tree grow poorly. Trees take enormous amounts of moisture and nutrients from the soil. So, if you can, select a garden site which is not in the root zone of trees. If you must encroach on the tree's territory, be aware that your garden will need extra moisture and fertilizer.

The problem for vegetables near any large tree is that of tree root competition. This varies with the type of tree. Pines are deep-rooted while oaks are shallow-rooted. A good way to tell where the root zone lies is to look carefully around the base of the tree in the summer, especially during periods of drought. You can spot the extent of the root penetration by the color, growth and appearance of grass or other plants already growing there. Remember the 'big guy' is going to get the good from the soil first.

THE IDEAL VEGETABLE SITE

Let us look again at the ideal vegetable site. Of all the criteria listed, the most important need is for at least six hours of full sun per day. Find those areas first. The second most important is drainage. Choose the sunniest area with the best drainage. Then choose the most level of the areas which conform to the first two criteria. Choose the richest, and then run the rows north and south if possible. And remember to avoid tree root zones if at all possible.

CHOOSING WHAT TO GROW

After choosing the site for your vegetable garden, you must now decide what to grow and where in the garden to put each crop. Some sort of garden plan is essential, for "willy-nilly" gardens seldom achieve their real potential. Garden plans can be the simplest of sketches or they can be quite detailed. I've learned about garden plans the hard way. For any number of reasons including pure laziness, I have often just gone to the garden and started planting. How would you like to have six rows of zucchini to harvest all summer? That's what happened to me one summer when I was "willy-nilly" planting. Another reason for a plan is that there is a tendency to plant everything at once so as to get on with the business of growing. This severely limits the variety of the garden and makes eating squash or okra or beans a real chore when everything matures at the same time. To make harvesting easier, try dividing your garden into various plots. Put this down on paper so that you'll be eating corn, beans, squash, and okra instead of just zucchini, like I did.

Everyone seems to want tomatoes, beans, squash, and corn, but these are by no means your only choices. There is much, much more. Look at this outstanding potential and then start making your garden plans.

SOUTHERN GARDENING SEASONS

Southern vegetable gardens have a twelve-month potential. There is hardly a day in the year when something cannot be taken from the garden. But this takes planning. Most of us think of the vegetable season as from frost to frost, that is, from the last frost of spring to the first frost of fall. Actually, you can start the vegetable garden in January with the first plantings of English peas. Then follows a whole succession of plantings through the winter, spring, summer, and fall.

The purist takes this one step further. The garden year starts in the fall, about the first of September in the South. However, let's be more practical in our thinking and start the garden year with the calendar.

WHEN TO PLANT	WHAT TYPE CROPS	WILL TAKE
January–February–Early March	Cold Weather	Hard Freeze
Mid March–Mid April	Cool Weather	Light Freeze
Mid April through Summer	Hot Weather	No Frost
Late August–September	Cool Weather	Light Freeze
Late September–October	Cold Weather	Hard Freeze

The author's winter garden

Corn and squash must wait for warm weather to plant.

Bib Lettuce will take frost but no freezes.

Onions are planted when the worst of the winter is over but while there is still danger of freezing weather.

Tomatoes need warm temperatures to develop well and to produce abundantly.

Smooth seeded English peas are planted when the weather is still cold.

GARDENING IN THE WINTER

The expression "dead of winter" aptly describes most of our feelings about the months of January and February. Our interest and feelings about gardening are often dead. My son says about me, "Dad's allergic to cold weather." I can make all the plans, order all the seed, dream of all the harvests, but can I work the garden when it's icy cold? No way! After all these years of gardening, it still takes a lot of push to get me into the garden in the dead of winter.

There is so much we can miss with this attitude that I have developed a little technique to fool my nature. Between Christmas and early January is usually an excellent gardening time. For some reason the weather is almost always milder at this time than toward the end of January and February. So I get inspired by perusing all the garden catalogs I can find, making all my charts, ordering my seed, and fooling myself into thinking that spring is almost here.

Then it is easy to get the tiller and head toward the garden, to turn under the green manure crops, lime the soil, and start the first plantings of English peas. Despite the bad weather that always follows, I have started my garden and I'm happy.

The good thing about my system is that there is something I can plant immediately: English peas. Not only do I start with the drudgery of tilling and liming, but I can do some of the fun work, which to me is *planting* something.

From here on out the garden is a going, growing place and a schedule is not so hard to follow. The "dead of winter" suddenly is a really tolerable time!

Timing becomes more important as spring gets closer and closer. To help you with your garden plans and planting, I have listed the crops with which you will have the best success during each season. After choosing the crops you think you would like to grow, turn to the description of

Plant English peas deep in
a furrow for protection.

these crops and how to grow each one. Make your cropping decisions from the information on when to grow each crop and the details about growing it. Factors like length of time to produce, amount of space needed, when you need the space for other more desirable crops, and the problems you might encounter, will all affect your decisions about each vegetable type. Remember, it would take a farm to grow every crop mentioned. This is where your garden plan comes in. The choice is now between you and your space, between what you like and the limitations set by the area in which you are going to garden.

WINTER COOL-WEATHER CROPS

Since very cold weather is always a threat in the beginning of our gardening year, the only vegetables safe to plant are the very hardy types and dormant perennial crops. Don't become over-enthusiastic and start planting cabbage in January. Stick to those crops which can take the icy blows when they come. You will have plenty of other work to do, like seeding in flats inside or in coldframes, planting the dormant perennial crops, and of course planting the few crops which can survive the Arctic-type fronts which the jet stream brings when it swings down too low.

In the dead of winter, take care when the weather warms, and it looks like spring. The calendar is usually right. January and early February may have balmy days, but it is best to leave cabbage and broccoli in the seed tray until the calendar says spring is near.

WINTER PLANTINGS

The following vegetables can stand almost any cold we have. After the danger of low-teens temperatures has passed, you can plant many other types of vegetables in the hardy class.

VERY HARDY CROPS	PERMANENT CROPS
HARDY ENGLISH PEA (smooth seed)	ASPARAGUS (roots)
ONION SET (button)	HORSERADISH (roots)
GARLIC (clove)	RHUBARB (roots)
	JERUSALEM ARTICHOKE

LATE WINTER—EARLY SPRING PLANTINGS

Hardy vegetables can be planted any time after the coldest low-teens temperatures have passed. They will take considerable cold and develop tougher plants with deeper roots if planted as soon as possible after the deep cold is over.

TYPE	PLANT FORM
IRISH POTATO	Pieces with eyes
ENGLISH PEA (wrinkled)	Seed
ONION	Seed
GREEN ONION	Seed or Plants
CABBAGE	Seed or Plants
BROCCOLI	Seed or Plants
BRUSSELS SPROUT	Seed or Plants
CAULIFLOWER	Seed or Plants
COLLARD	Seed or Plants
KALE	Seed or Plants
KOHLRABI	Seed or Plants

SPRING COOL-WEATHER CROPS

By the end of February and in the early part of March, there is still danger of cold weather, but the air is "softer" and the onrushing cold less extreme. This is the time to really start the early spring-planted crops.

You can plant these types of vegetables while there is danger of frosts and freezes. But for best results, plant them as the weather begins to moderate and, though freezing temperatures might occur, when you no longer expect temperatures in the low twenties and teens.

TYPE	PLANT FROM SEED	FROM PLANTS
BEET & SWISS CHARD	Seed	
CARROT	Seed	
CELERY & CELERIAC	Seed	
CRESS	Seed	
ENDIVE	Seed	
ESCAROLE	Seed	
LETTUCE, LEAF	Seed	Plants
LETTUCE, ICEBERG TYPE	Seed	Plants
MUSTARD	Seed	
PARSLEY	Seed	Plants
PARSNIP	Seed	
RADISH	Seed	
RAPEGREEN	Seed	
RUTABAGA	Seed	
SALSIFY	Seed	
SPINACH	Seed	
TURNIP	Seed	

Planting eggplant too early invites attacks of flea beetles.

Spreading one of the new porous polyvinyl nets over the row helps to protect young germinating seeds and seedlings.

WARM-WEATHER CROPS

In early April with the passing of the last danger of frost, we have only one real consideration: the temperature of the soil. Now the tops of our plants are largely safe, but many seeds are not happy in cold, wet soil. In fact, seeds of sweet corn, okra, cow peas, and large-seeded types like pumpkins and watermelons are liable to rot in wet ground before they germinate. Sweet potato slips just won't grow, peppers stunt, and eggplant are attacked by hordes of flea beetles (they also might stunt). By early May the ground has warmed and night temperatures are high enough so that you can plant all those problem plants.

SPRING PLANTINGS AFTER FROST

These plants cannot stand frost on the growing plant, but the seed will germinate before the ground temperature rises into the upper sixties and low seventies. In the South, the traditional bean-planting date was on Good Friday. This was thought to be the last frost date, since it comes at the time of the full moon nearest the spring equinox. You will need to identify the average date of the last killing frost of the season and plant after that date.

TYPE	PLANT FORM
BEAN, BUSH SNAP	Seed
BEAN, POLE SNAP	Seed
BEAN, SOY	Seed
CANTALOUPE	Seed
CORN, ROASTING EAR	Seed
CORN, POP	Seed
HONEYDEW	Seed
TOMATO	Seed or Plants

LATE SPRING—EARLY SUMMER PLANTINGS

These crops cannot germinate well in cold wet soil even though the days may be warm. Therefore, after the danger of frost has passed, wait for the ground to begin to warm before planting.

TYPE	PLANT FORM
BEAN, LIMA	Seed
CORN, SWEET	Seed
CUCUMBER	Seed
SQUASH	Seed
WATERMELON	Seed

EARLY SUMMER PLANTINGS

These types of vegetables do best when both the ground and the air are warm. If peppers and eggplant don't have a nighttime temperature in the sixties, the plants will "stunt," become tough and hard, and grow poorly. Later planting of these two will reduce the frequency of flea beetle attacks and save much time dusting or spraying to control them.

TYPE	PLANT FORM
COWPEA	Seed
EGGPLANT	Plants
GOURD	Seed
OKRA	Seed
PEANUT	Seed
PEPPER	Plants
PUMPKIN	Seed
SWEET POTATO	Plants

REPEAT PLANTINGS

Many of the vegetables planted after the danger of frost will produce well if planted even later. There is a great advantage in planting crops like corn several times so that you are not covered up with corn for a short period of time and then finished. The crops which are particularly adapted to repeat plantings are those with a concentrated fruit set. Beans, corn, squash, cucumber, and even tomatoes can be planted continuously into June.

FALL COOL-WEATHER CROPS

Though many of us end our gardening after harvesting our spring-planted crops, we should consider extending the harvest by planting for fall.

Many hardy spring crops may be planted again in late August and early September for another crop in October and November. This is a particularly fulfilling time for harvest and an easy crop to grow. The ground is usually in good shape and there should be a lot of residual fertilizer left.

TYPE	PLANT FORM
BEET	Seed
BROCCOLI	Seed or Plants
CABBAGE	Plants
CARROT	Seed
CAULIFLOWER	Plants
COLLARD	Seed or Plants
GARLIC	Cloves
KALE	Seed or Plants
KOHLRABI	Seed or Plants
LETTUCE, LEAF	Seed or Plants
MUSTARD	Seed
ONION	Seed, Sets, or Plants
PARSLEY	Seed or Plants
RADISH	Seed
RAPEGREEN	Seed
SHALLOT	Bulbs
SPINACH	Seed
SWISS CHARD	Seed
TURNIP	Seed

OVERWINTERING VEGETABLES

You can plant some of the more hardy vegetables in late September and October so they will grow through the cold winter and produce very early crops next year. They do not all make it through each winter, especially if the winters are so severe that the temperatures dip below zero. But the results are so rewarding that you should try them every year.

The vegetables which do very well almost every year are the onion-garlic, sweet onions, storing onions, shallots, and green bunching onions for salads. It takes a rare winter to wipe out these great treats.

The very hardy cabbages will also survive most winters, as well as their close cousins, kale and collards.

Asparagus, a perennial crop which
lasts for many years in the
Southern garden.

MULTI-SEASON CROPS

All of the plants we have talked about are one-season plants or, correctly
speaking, annuals. However, some of our potential vegetable plants are
multi-season crops or perennials. These are a very important part of the
Southern vegetable potential. Do not overlook these fabulous plants when
planning your vegetable garden. Asparagus, horseradish, rhubarb,
Jerusalem artichokes, and even globe artichokes will greatly enhance the
quality of your production!

ADAPTING YOUR SITE TO THE SEASON

From these basic facts you can start a cropping plan. But before bringing
out pencil, paper, and notebook, take another look at the garden site. If
your garden is only marginally sunny for the main summer crops, the sunlight may be much better for growing vegetables in the early spring or fall
when leaves from the surrounding deciduous trees are off the trees or
when the sun is in the Southern sky.

Trees may shade the garden during one season but not during another since the sun
moves in the sky.

You will notice that the early spring garden has some very definite advantages. The leaves of oaks, poplars, and maples are really not a serious problem until the end of April or early May. Therefore, you can grow many early, quick crops like beets in areas which are too shady for squash. The squash will not be planted until the end of April when the heavy deciduous shade is over that part of the garden.

In the fall the leaf cover stays on most trees until it is too late for most cool-season crops, so there is not the advantage in the fall that there is in the spring.

SEASONS FOR INSECTS AND DISEASES

It is important to consider timing before you make your final garden plan, especially in relationship to insects and diseases. Think of the flea beetle and eggplant, for instance. If eggplant is set out very early, the cool nights are ideal for the development of flea beetles. If you wait until the nights are warm to plant, you can contain the flea beetle attacks with good insect control measures which won't break the bank.

For years I tried to have sequential plantings of sweet corn, always with very poor success. Then I found that sweet corn planted from the end of April through May is bothered very little by earworms and stalk borers. But later plantings, from mid to late June, are almost impossible to keep free from these destructive worms.

Other late summer pests are white fly, mildew, and spider mites. April and May plantings of insect-susceptible plants like squash and cucumbers are problem-free, but June and July plantings are a mess. Maybe that's good, because by the end of the summer I've eaten enough squash and cucumbers to be ready for a breather.

Follow your own previous gardening experiences, or if you are a beginner in vegetable gardening, use these guidelines to develop a good cropping plan. Now you can get your notebook and start your vegetable garden plan.

Sweet corn planted in mid-summer is more subject to stalk borers and ear worms.

Cabbage planted too late in the spring matures after the cabbage worms appear.

DEVELOPING YOUR CROP PLAN

With all the preliminaries out of the way, it is time to start developing your garden plan. You've chosen your garden site and you know the seasons during which you can be successful. The fun starts with the development of your future garden on paper.

I like to sit down with a notebook and just start dreaming, listing all the vegetables I want to grow, season by season: first, the winter and early spring-planted crops, then the mid-spring, then the early summer, and finally the late summer and fall.

Perhaps your garden site doesn't allow you to have a winter garden or a fall garden. Now is the time to determine when you can plant and harvest. Choose the seasons you are going to garden as carefully as you choose the vegetables you are going to grow. One determines the fate of the other.

The choice of the crops follows the choice of the seasons. The vegetable description section is designed to give the information necessary to choose wisely. If you are strictly a tomato, pepper, eggplant, squash, and cucumber (or another tender crop) gardener, you know that your garden must be ready to plant in April. If you are going to plant only in February and March, you know your crop choice will be limited to such things as Irish potatoes, onions, cabbage, and broccoli.

Now list a time for planting each crop. Timing is extremely important in the garden. A one- or two-week variance may mean the difference between success or failure. In the old days the almanac determined when to plant. You planted root crops on the wane of the moon, and fruit and leaf crops on the wax of the moon. Sound silly? Perhaps, but it made you plant at a given time each year and that is why old-time gardeners were so successful. They always stayed on a schedule.

Now that your list and times for planting are complete, you should lay out the garden. Make your plan fit your garden as exactly as possible. Have the rows run in the same direction on paper as they will run in the garden. Have them the same length with the same spacing between rows that will be in the garden, and the same number of rows on paper as you will be able to plant in the garden.

Crop plans may be very simple or very detailed. I have found, after gardening in the same spot for so long, that my garden plans are simpler than they used to be. The reason is easy to see. I've done it so many times that I know how many rows are in each plot, and I know that row number 6 of plot 3 will give me enough beans, and so forth. Thus, my plans are row listings rather than an actual graph. But as you start a new garden site, draw it the more detailed way at first and you will be surprised how much it helps.

CHAPTER 2

VEGETABLES FOR THE SOUTH

The earliest gardens of history were more functional than aesthetic. Cultivated areas around the home were used to grow food for use on the table and not flowers for vases. The kitchen garden, the herb garden, and the fruit garden were necessary for variety and nutrition; flowers were for kings and princes, in the main, and not for the cottage garden. Beauty did become important later, and flowers became mixed with vegetables, herbs, and fruits because the spirit plays such an important role in the lives of men. The emphasis remained for many centuries, however, on productivity, and early gardeners in this country continued the tradition of growing food for the table.

The South is blessed with a bounteous potential for producing all of the most delicious varieties of vegetables. No matter what type of soil you have, how large your growing area is, or how much time you have to garden, you are sure to find a vegetable here to suit your taste and grace your table.

ALL ABOUT VEGETABLES FOR THE SOUTH

ARTICHOKE
Cynara Scolymus

HISTORY

This is one of the most delightful vegetables of the permanent garden. Frankly, I had never given its culture much thought, believing that it was a plant for more cool and humid climates as are found in the Burgundy region of France. Not until we lived in Egypt did the culture of artichokes begin to have much appeal. I found that the Nile Delta is filled with artichokes, which proved that very hot temperatures are perfectly satisfactory for growing them. On the Mediterranean coast of Morocco, which also has its share of heat, the artichoke is widely grown for home and commercial consumption. It makes sense for us to grow this plant in the South because it is a native of southern Europe and the Canary Islands.

I found references to its cultivation as far back as 1675 (*The French Gardiner,* by John Evelyn, Esq., published in London) and its cultivation probably dates back to Roman times. William White, in his *Gardening for The South,* published in 1868, describes it as a crop which ". . . is wholesome, yet contains but little nutriment and is cultivated merely to please the palate."

White describes the English way of peeling the boiled leaves from the globe at the table and dipping the fleshy base into "butter and pepper." Of course, these days most people prefer Hollandaise sauce. In Egypt they seldom eat the leaves but cultivate the chokes for the "hearts" which they cook and stuff with delightful meats. In my mind, artichokes certainly do delight the palate.

FORMS AVAILABLE

Good seed and slips of artichokes are hard to find, but some of the better mail order houses do list them. You can often find *Green Globe,* though I prefer *Violetta,* which is not nearly as common. Any are worth a try!

It is best to obtain suckers of high quality varieties, though you can use good seed if "slips" are unavailable.

PLANTING AND GROWING

Artichokes should be grown in the richest, loamiest part of the garden. Clay should be enriched to accommodate this specific need. Ground pine bark, peat moss, and ample amounts of humus are all necessary to prepare a good artichoke bed.

Start seed in January inside or in a hot bed, and transplant to pots as soon as the true leaves appear. Grow them into stocky plants for transplanting when the danger of a heavy freeze has passed. You can also order "slips" or suckers to arrive as soon as the coldest weather has finished and plant directly in the open ground.

The artichokes should be planted 3 feet apart in rows 4 feet apart. After enriching the soil, apply a 10-10-10 fertilizer as a pre-plant application. Keep plants growing with additional side dressings of the 10-10-10, but after the globes first appear, do not fertilize again.

Artichokes need moisture and should be grown in soil that will hold moisture but drains off excess amounts. It is wise, here in the South, to plant them on beds so that you can irrigate the furrows when it is dry. Overhead sprinkler-type irrigation invites trouble and should be avoided.

The first year you may have a few chokes in the late summer or early fall, but they may be small, especially if you started the plants from seed. The second year is the first good crop. The bed will continue to flourish until about the fifth year. Then you should take up the plants in the spring when the new shoots are starting, separate them, and reset them in a new location.

Many people find that it is wise after the third year to remove several shoots from each clump and start a new bed with them to prevent a loss of one year when resetting the whole bed.

❦ JERUSALEM ARTICHOKE
Helianthus tuberosus

HISTORY

The Jerusalem artichoke belies its name. Neither does it come from Jerusalem nor is it an artichoke. It is, rather, a tuber-forming member of the sunflower family which came, reportedly, originally from Brazil. It was grown in 17th-century Europe as a good source of carbohydrate but was replaced by the much tastier potato. It has hung on in Southern gardens mainly as a delicious pickled delicacy and as a wonderful food for hogs. I have never seen or heard of it used by humans as anything but a pickled delicacy, though *Hortus Third* reports that it is a commercial source of inulin (white polysaccharide) and a good diabetic food. So there is yet hope for it as a table dish and not just as food for pigs.

PLANTING AND GROWING

One thing is certain. The Jerusalem artichoke is easy to grow and even may become a weed problem. It is grown like potatoes but does not need as rich a soil. Plant the tubers in spring in beds at the edge of the garden to keep it from becoming a pest. Grow it through the fall and dig just before the first hard freeze. Separate the tubers from the stems and store them in a cool dry place just as you store potatoes. When you are digging, if you leave a few of the tubers in the bed and mulch the bed with leaves, you will not need to replant in the spring because the tubers will overwinter and rejuvenate the bed.

The only problem that I have observed is that if you do not rework the ground each year, perennial weeds may become a serious problem. Total removal of the tubers in the fall allows you to work the bed each year and keep a cleaner, more attractive garden.

Globe Artichoke

Mary Washington Asparagus

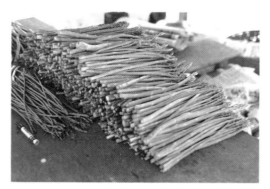

Fresh-cut asparagus

Early spring spears of asparagus

The first commercial crop of asparagus ever grown in modern Egypt. EAACO project, West Nobaria, Egypt

Wooden trellises to keep heavily growing asparagus from falling over

Don Hastings III side dressing our asparagus bed

❦ ASPARAGUS
❦ *Asparagus officinalis*

HISTORY

Asparagus is one of the most elegant crops we can grow. It is permanent, productive, and a real delight to the home gardener. In the Middle East they don't eat it; in England they call it grass; in the United States it is a real delicacy. On the European continent it is almost always eaten in the white, blanched form, while here and in England the green shoots are preferred.

Asparagus has been a cultivated plant for at least 2,000 years. William White says that Cato gave a full account of its cultivation in 150 B.C., and the Emperor Augustus was supposed to be particularly partial to it. It is found growing wild through most of the coastal parts of Europe, North Africa, and the Mid-East. Its culture may have started in Greece, where much has been written of its delicacy. John Abercrombie in *Abercrombie's Practical Gardener*, published in 1823 in London, specifically states that it is native to Britain and gives extensive directions for its cultivation.

When I was a child, my mother and I would walk the terraces of several of our fields with a bucket to cut fresh asparagus which had naturalized on these ditch banks and always seemed to grow better there than in the garden. This gift from nature was there for the taking. She always said the Lord knew much better ways of growing things than we humans did.

Asparagus is a good home crop despite the effort it takes to get a good bed started. Once you get it established, you will have great rewards. Though this may be just my personal preference, I think the white asparagus had best be left to the commercial growers. It is a lot of trouble, and anyway the green is delicious.

FORMS AVAILABLE

You can start asparagus from seed or from roots. The home gardener usually does better with the roots because it saves considerable time until the first cuttings may be made. Recently, catalogs have advertised two- and three-year crowns; the advantage of the older crowns is the additional savings in time before the first cutting.

Mary Washington has long been the best variety since it is highly rust-resistant. Recently, the University of California has been doing some hybridizing of asparagus to produce more vigorous crops which may be cut sooner. However, none of these seem to be as rust-resistant as *Mary Washington,* and here in the South, rust can really be a problem during "dog days" in the summer. *Brock's Imperial Hybrid* is said to be somewhat rust-resistant and can be tried on a limited basis.

PLANTING AND GROWING

An asparagus bed is a more or less permanent part of the garden. A good bed will last at least 12 years, so take care in choosing a place. Asparagus requires loose, well-drained soil which holds enough moisture to produce large, tender spikes quickly. You can grow asparagus either in a rich well-drained part of the garden in deep furrows or, if the ground tends to be dry, in beds so that furrow irrigation is possible. Some very successful beds are built with cross ties and filled with well-rotted leaves and other humus material.

First plow, till, or turn very deeply the whole asparagus area. Add large amounts of well-rotted humus, manure, peat moss, and ground bark to enrich the soil and allow for drainage and good moisture-holding capacity. Asparagus needs moisture but cannot develop in poorly drained soil.

I prefer to grow asparagus in raised beds 3 feet across, with a distance of 6 feet from the center of one bed to the center of the next. The bed should be at least 18 inches deep. After the beds are all made, open a furrow in the middle of each bed about 8 inches deep and about 1 foot wide. Make a small ridge in the bottom of each furrow. Plant the crowns with the roots spread out and down over this ridge. Cover the plants with the loose well-prepared soil taken from the furrow. The top of the crown should be covered about two inches with loose soil. As the new shoots develop, continue drawing loose soil against the stems until the planting furrow has been completely filled. In particularly heavy clay you may fill the furrow with well-rotted compost.

Plant seedlings in much the same way, except make the furrow only about half as deep. For spring seedlings, start seed inside in January and pot the seedlings, moving them into a cooler place as the young fronds develop. Keep the young potted plants fertilized with a liquid fertilizer to obtain tough little plants for setting after the danger of a hard freeze has passed.

Do not cut asparagus the first season no matter what form you planted. Keep the plants cleanly cultivated and well watered to maximize the growth. After the fronds have died in the fall, remove them and cover the bed with manure or compost.

The second season can be the first harvest from crown plantings, but if you overdo the cutting, you will weaken the plants. You may cut over a period of about six weeks (about half the spears). After that, leave the other half of the spears to develop into fern fronds. In subsequent years, you can harvest spears until the first seed balls appear. Then stop harvesting to allow the plants to build back their strength.

Do not cut back plants grown from seed until the third season.

The secret of good asparagus production is plenty of moisture and rich, well-fertilized soil. Asparagus grown in dry conditions will be weak, small, and tough. Growing asparagus in raised beds allows for furrow irrigation. When the weather is very dry, merely fill the furrow between the rows with water and allow it to soak slowly into the beds. Fertilizing with a high nitrogen fertilizer will push the growth of the spears and make them larger. Apply a 10-10-10 fertilizer in the spring and about every two months during the growing season. If the growth is not as rapid as you want, you may side-dress with ammonium nitrate between the 10-10-10 applications.

BEANS

Beans are one of the most widely grown food sources in the world today. In the poorer nations, mature dried beans are one of the sources of protein which literally keep the population alive. Some of the youngsters on our desert farm in Egypt ate almost no other food besides the foule bean which is so common in that country. Along with pita bread, they ate this bean at almost every meal in one form or another. It gave us Americans a tremendous sense of accomplishment to see the impact on their health and growth which came when they added to their diet the fresh tomatoes, melons, and other produce from our fields.

The term "bean" encompasses many different plants in the legume family which are native to most of the world. They were known in antiquity, and were commonly cultivated in England in the 17th century. Evelyn describes in detail the practices of planting beans, the main type being the Marsh bean, a large, flat bean of pale color. The Marsh was the *Vicia Faba* which Abercrombie stated came from Egypt. More probably it came from somewhat east of the Nile and found its way to Europe. This is the bean known also as the broad bean or Windsor bean, and bears little resemblance to our garden bean.

Fortunately we in the South can grow a wide range of beans. The bush snap bean of the garden is perhaps the greatest treasure, but there are many others which add great variety.

Bailey in *The Standard Cyclopedia of Horticulture* designates five major classes of beans:

- Broad bean, *Vicia Faba*
- Kidney bean, *Phaseolus vulgaris*
- Lima bean, *Phaseolus lunatus* and *P. limensis*
- Dolichos bean, *Dolichos* sp.
- Soya bean, *Glycine hispida* (now *Glycine Max*)

He also listed a number of other less important beans, like the *Scarlet Runner* bean which is often used as an ornament.

In addition, all sorts of horticultural plants have the name "bean" attached. Some, like the old Southern favorite "Yard Long Bean" (*Vigna unquiculata* subsp. *sesquipedalis*) have had some gardener acceptance.

For the Southern gardener most attention is placed on the *Phaseolus vulgaris* or kidney bean which encompasses all our bush and pole snap beans, and *Phaseolus limensis* and *lunatus* which include all our lima beans. The others are novelties and should be planted for fun but not necessarily for their horticultural value.

Beans are easy to grow and can be planted as soon as the danger of frost has passed. Grow them in successive crops because most varieties and types have a concentrated fruit set and soon are finished. Plant part of a row at a time, about every two weeks, to have continuous harvest until frost.

Pole snap beans are an exception to this generality. Plant pole beans in the spring, stake them well, keep them growing with continuous fertilizing, and watch the vines bear until late summer, possibly even until frost.

BUSH SNAP BEAN
Phaseolus vulgaris

FORMS AVAILABLE

Since beans are so universally grown, there are tremendous numbers of varieties from which to choose. I am sure there are many special ones from the good old days which have particular appeal to you. Fortunately, beans are one crop which technology has not "ruined" by overemphasizing a characteristic to the advantage of the commercial grower, but not good for the home gardener. The improvement in quality has been outstanding. Today beans are truly stringless even when the seeds are quite well formed and fiber content in the pod is low.

All in all, today's bean varieties are in every way excellent.

BUSH SNAP BEAN VARIETIES
Plant 1 lb. per 100 Feet of Row

VARIETY	DAYS TO MATURITY	SPECIAL FEATURES
BLUE LAKE 141*	56	Long season
CONTENDER*	48	Disease resistance (mosaic & mildew)
COMMODORE	58	Bush Kentucky Wonder
BLUE LAKE 274	55	Concentrated set (for freezing)
STRIKE*	52	Very high yields
ROMA II	60	Distinctive taste, flat beans

*My favorites

PLANTING AND GROWING

The bush snap beans are perhaps the easiest of all crops of the garden. They require little except proper fertilizing before planting and clean cultivation. They are a fast crop, many coming to harvest within 50 days of the sprouted seed. Plant successive crops to give continuous harvest until frost, since most commonly-grown varieties have a fairly concentrated fruit set.

Prepare the area in which bush snap beans are to be planted in early- to mid-March. Lime the soil well and work it as deeply as possible. The addition of humus, especially green manure from a legume, is very helpful.

As soon as the danger of the last frost has passed, plant snap beans. Traditionally, bush and pole snap beans were planted in the South on Good Friday since this is the time of the first full moon after the spring equinox, and always seems to bring a cold snap. If beans are planted this day, the seed will be germinating after the last frost. Be careful, though, because your particular location may have a killing frost somewhat later. Sprouted beans cannot withstand frost and they should not be up and growing when there is danger of a frosty night.

I prefer to plant early beans on a bed because planting in the water furrow when the ground is still cold may cause problems with germination. When you are ready to plant, make each bed about 2 feet across with the beds placed 3 feet apart. The beds should be at least 18 inches deep. After preparing the beds, draw out a 4-inch deep furrow in the top of the bed. Dust lightly with a 10-10-10

Contender Bean

Strike Bean

Commodore, Bush Kentucky Wonder Bean

Roma Bean

Scarlet Runner Beans, an ornamental
as well as a vegetable

Young bean
seedlings off to
a good start

29

Watch out for rabbits. They love early beans.

Beans dying because of poor drainage

Blue Lake Pole Bean

Mexican Bean Beetles

Single pole supports for pole beans

fertilizer in the bottom of this furrow. Now draw some loose soil over the fertilizer, making sure that all the raw 10-10-10 is incorporated in the soil and that none will come into contact with the germinating seed. This furrow should now be about 1 to 2 inches deep. Drop the bean seed in the bottom of this furrow, spacing the seed about 2 inches apart. Now draw loose soil into the furrow until it is filled.

When the seeds have germinated, thin the crop so that the plants are spaced 8 inches apart in the row.

Keep beans cleanly cultivated and free from weed and grass competition. Beans are legumes and will manufacture nitrate nitrogen from the air. But they should never be allowed to lack nutrients. Watch the color of the leaves as the plants develop. They should be a rich, dark green and as the heavy set of fruit develops, correct any lightening of the color immediately with a light side-dressing of 10-10-10 fertilizer.

Pick beans frequently to prevent the pods from overdeveloping and becoming tough, stringy and, in my opinion, useless. Clean picking will also encourage continued bloom and a longer bearing season. I prefer eating snap beans which are extremely small and tender, and I try to harvest when they are no larger than the diameter of a pencil.

PROBLEMS

There are a number of insects and diseases which attack garden beans. Early plantings seldom are bothered too greatly, and all you usually need is a regular dusting with Sevin. However, be aware of bean beetles and rust. If they appear, check with your County Extension Service for the latest recommendations of safe controls.

In addition, rabbits can be a disaster, particularly in the spring. These little four-legged friends love to feast on young beans with three or four sets of leaves. I have had row after row eaten to the stem. It is a most discouraging sight to see your garden beans stripped of the leaves. One year I even planted a row of lettuce between the beans and the woods. These furry critters hopped right over my lettuce and stripped the beans down to the stem.

I have tried just about everything to keep the rabbits away, including a strong portion of hot pepper juice. The only repellent which has been in any way satisfactory is human hair. I got sacks of hair from the barber shop and put it in bunches around the garden about every two feet. No rabbits ate my beans, or anything else.

POLE SNAP BEAN
Phaseolus vulgaris

Pole snap beans are excellent for any garden which has the space. These beans will produce over a much longer period than bush snap beans and provide a continuous supply of fresh beans for the table from first crop to frost. They have the same good taste and stringless quality as the bush snap beans.

FORMS AVAILABLE

POLE SNAP BEAN VARIETIES
Plant ½ lb. per 100 Feet of Row

VARIETY	DAYS TO MATURITY	SPECIAL FEATURES
BLUE LAKE*	65	Very long season
KENTUCKY WONDER	65	Distinctive flavor, flattened pod
ALABAMA #1	65	Purple bean, nematode-resistant
DADE (IMPROVED MCCASLAN)*	60	Rust and mosaic resistant

*My recommendations

PLANTING AND GROWING

The only extra requirement for pole beans is space; they do grow large! And you must provide something on which they can grow.

Most homeowners use bamboo poles for the support. The poles should be strong and at least 8 feet long, preferably 10. But you can use other methods. I have seen pole beans grown on everything from an ornamental arbor to a four-sided metal clothes-drying frame. Chain link fences will work as well as strings hanging from tall fences and walls. All that is really necessary is something for the vines to twine around which is tall enough for the very longest vines.

No matter what you use, the planting requirements are about the same. Work the soil and prepare it as for bush beans. Except for early spring plantings which grow better in raised beds, it is best to plant the bean seeds in hills, though I have used both methods when growing in the garden proper and supporting with bamboo poles.

My best results with pole beans have been from growing two rows side by side, tying the tops of two poles, one from each row together, over the furrow between. Using this method requires little extra work. Prepare the garden first by tilling and liming. For early spring planting, use the bed method with the beds 2 feet wide and 3 feet apart as with bush beans. Then top-dress the beds with 10-10-10 fertilizer. Set the poles at an angle so that the tops meet over the middle. Tie the poles together about a foot from the tops, making a "v" at the top. Set the poles as deep as possible to keep them standing in wind and rain, 3 feet apart in the row. After you have set the two rows of poles and tied them over the middle, take another ten-foot pole and lay it across the "v's" parallel to the ground. Now tie this horizontal support pole to each "v." Continue with these support poles until there is one connected to each of the uprights. When this is finished, it is wise to run a strong line from the top of the first and last poles in each row to a well-set ground stake. This will prevent wind from blowing down the row and toppling all your hard work like dominoes.

Kentucky Wonder Pole Bean

Bridgeton, small green lima bean

Small garden bean support

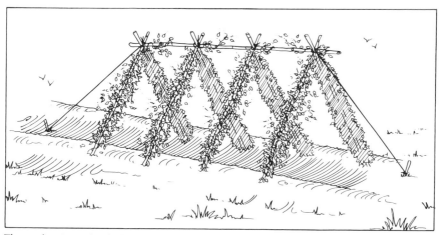

The author's method of training beans

Now open a hole and plant about four pole bean seed beside the foot of each pole. These will sprout and start climbing up each pole. If you do not make a bed, as described above, be sure to plant these seed in a hill. The base of the stakes or the hills should be 3 feet apart in the row.

You will need a regular fertilizer program to keep the pole beans growing and producing. After the original application of the 10-10-10 fertilizer, I prefer to use a 6-12-12 or a 5-10-15 for growth and fruiting during the harvest season.

Harvest pole beans just as you do bush snap beans: frequently. It is vitally important to encourage new blooms which will set the new beans by picking the maturing crop as soon as it is ready.

In the old days, it was common to plant corn and pole beans at the same time so that the corn stalks would act as the support for the beans. There were several old favorite pole bean varieties ideal for the purpose because they were long maturing. This allowed the corn to ripen before the beans covered the stalks. The corn used was, of course, field corn which grew tall and had heavy stalks. Growing modern pole beans on corn is possible but not nearly as satisfactory since the common sweet corn of today's gardens is much smaller growing and the stalks are hardly strong enough to support a heavy-growing bean vine.

I have seen some success using beans in *Trucker's Favorite Roasting Ear* corn. The best variety of good pole snap beans would be *Blue Lake*, which matures in about 65 days. Since *Trucker's Favorite* matures in over 75 days, the pole beans should not be planted at the same time as the corn, but planted about ten days after the corn has come up. There are some old-fashioned *Cornfield* beans which take over 70 days and might possibly be obtained from a farm supply store. But *Cornfield* beans are stringy and somewhat fibrous when they mature.

Silver Queen sweet corn is the most common variety grown in the South today. The stalk is somewhat heavier than most other varieties of sweet corn, but unless it is grown in particularly rich soil and fertilized heavily, it is not strong enough to support most beans.

There is an alternative, however; that is to plant a half-runner bean like the variety *State*, since it needs some support, but its vines are not too adventurous or heavy growing. Half-runner beans are not as fine quality as *Blue Lake*, since they are stringy if allowed to mature too long. But *State* is very good for freezing.

PROBLEMS

Since pole beans take longer to grow than bush beans, you should be constantly on guard for attacks from bean beetles and diseases. On some varieties of pole beans, rust is a particular problem. Check your County Extension Service bulletins for the best chemicals to use.

🌱 LIMA BEAN
🌰 *Phaseolus limensis* and *lunatus*

HISTORY

Lima beans are grown for their immature seeds which, when harvested and cooked, are a delightful dish. They seem to have originated in the tropical Western

Hemisphere, probably Brazil. They have been a part of American vegetable gardening, especially in the South, since the 1700s.

FORMS AVAILABLE

There are two distinct types, both grown widely. The first is the common lima bean, represented by such varieties as *King-of-the-Garden* Pole Lima and *Fordhook* Bush Lima. The second is the Carolina or sieva bean that is now more commonly known as the Butterbean. This type includes the small limas like *Henderson* Bush Lima and *Dixie Butterpea*, and the more recent varieties like *Bridgeton* and *Cangreen*.

Nowadays few pole lima beans are grown in the home garden because the excellent bush varieties produce ample harvests over a long period of time and do not necessitate the trouble of staking.

BUSH LIMA BEAN VARIETIES
Plant 1 lb. per 100 Feet of Row

VARIETY	DAYS TO MATURITY	SPECIAL FEATURES
BRIDGETON*	60	High disease resistance, early, green seed
HENDERSON	65	White seed, small
DIXIE BUTTERPEA	75	Rounded white seed, small seed
JACKSON WONDER	65	Small, speckled seed

*My favorite

POLE LIMA BEAN VARIETIES
Plant ½ lb. per 100 Feet of Row

VARIETY	DAYS TO MATURITY	SPECIAL FEATURES
KING-OF-THE-GARDEN	88	Large white lima
CHRISTMAS	84	White with red seed
SIEVA	80	Seed are pale green

PLANTING AND GROWING

Lima beans take longer to come into bearing than snap beans and are less hardy. Soil preparation for lima beans is similar to that of snap beans. Do not plant them in cold wet soil but only after the weather has warmed. I have found that planting in beds 2 feet wide with two rows to the bed is ideal for the bush varieties. The beds should be far enough apart (at least 2½ feet) to allow clean cultivation. If you plant in beds, you can plant slightly earlier since the beds keep the seed from being down in the cold, wet water furrow where they would probably rot. Plant the seed of the bush varieties 1 to 1½ inches deep and spaced 2 to 3 inches apart.

After they germinate, thin the plants so that they are 8 inches apart. Plant pole lima beans in hills or at the base of the stakes on the bed, just like pole snap beans. Use the same 3-foot spacings between hills or stakes.

Keep lima beans growing well but do not over-fertilize. If you do, the plants will grow extremely rank and produce low yields. Start with a pre-plant 10-10-10 just as with snap beans, but do not give additional fertilizer unless you see the plant is light in color and growing poorly. If it is, side-dress with a 6-12-12 or 5-10-15 formula.

Keep all lima beans cleanly picked. If you allow the pods to dry on the vine, you will reduce the number of flowers being set and reduce your future harvests.

Other Beans

There are a number of lesser beans that may have some interest as novelties in the garden. The scarlet runner bean is grown primarily as an ornament, and the old-fashioned yard-long bean is grown more for fun, though the long beans are edible if they are harvested before they become tough.

These and other minor beans are grown in the basic manner described above for regular garden beans. Before attempting to grow these unusual beans, be certain whether they are bush or climbing types so that you may provide the proper growing environment.

The economically and horticulturally important bean, *Soya* bean, will be discussed later.

BEET
Beta vulgaris

HISTORY

The beet is one of our most successful crops. It is easy to grow during the cool seasons, and it matures quickly. Though the spring crop is most often grown, do not overlook the opportunity of growing beets in the fall.

The original beet is found growing wild on sandy lands by the sea from the Atlantic coast of North Africa across to the Caspian Sea and Persia. This native had a long root and its resemblance to the modern beet is more botanical than practical. The predecessor of today's beet probably appeared in upper Europe in the 16th century. Though Sturtevant gives references to a long-rooted beet as early as 1493, the rounded beet did not seem to appear until the 16th century. I found references in John Evelyn's treatise to the "Red Beet or Roman Parsnep" in 1675. Abercrombie gave it much space in 1823, and by then a number of varieties had evolved, including *Swiss Chard*.

The sugar beet, which is closely related to the garden beet, is becoming more prized as an economic plant, especially in countries where sugar cane cannot be grown. It is rarely grown in the garden except as a novelty.

BEET VARIETIES
Sow 1 Ounce per 50 Feet of Row

VARIETY	DAYS TO MATURITY	SPECIAL FEATURES
DETROIT DARK RED	58	Dark red, globe-shaped
RUBY QUEEN	52	Bright red, round-shaped

PLANTING AND GROWING

Beets must be grown when the weather is cool; otherwise, the quality of the root is poor. Hot weather beets are fibrous and lack the sweetness of those which mature when the weather is cool. Sow beets in the spring as soon as the hard freezes have finished, and fall crop beets in early September.

In addition, beets require a loose, loamy soil to produce a well-formed vegetable. Tight, sticky clay causes poor root formation and prevents good results.

Work the soil deeply, adding well-rotted humus, ground bark, or any other soil amendment which will loosen the soil and prevent compaction.

Grow beets in raised beds which are 2 feet across, with 3 feet between the beds to accommodate a tiller for cultivation. Top-dress the beds with a 10-10-10 fertilizer and work it in with a potato hook or a bow rake. Make two shallow furrows 12 inches apart on the bed. Plant seed 1/2 to 1 inch deep. Sow seed 1/2 to 1 inch apart to insure a good stand.

You can allow the beets to develop a short top before you thin them, and then you can use the tops from these thinnings for beet greens, a delicious boiled dish. Thin plants to 6-inch spacings for the double row beds or 4-inch spacings for the single row beds.

If the plants need additional fertilizer during their heavy growth time, apply a light side-dressing of 10-10-10 about halfway through the growth period.

Always keep the soil worked around beets. Frequent tilling of the middles and culture of the beds with a hand cultivator will prevent compaction and poor root development.

Beets should be harvested before they are too large; the ideal size is 3 to 4 inches across.

 BROCCOLI
Brassica oleracea, Botrytis Group

HISTORY

Broccoli is one of my favorite vegetables. It is easy to grow in the South, ideal for the spring and the fall, and produces extraordinarily well. I have found it a far superior plant and much easier to grow than its close relative the cauliflower. And

Ruby Queen Beet

Cleopatra Broccoli

Side shoots of broccoli develop after the main head has been cut.

Green Duke Broccoli harvested by an Egyptian girl.

frankly, I don't think that any cauliflower ever cooked could hold a candle to this delicious vegetable.

Broccoli may date back to Roman times, but there is no proof. It probably came from Italy into Europe proper in the 17th or 18th century. Yet even to this day it takes a back seat to cauliflower in most of Europe except, perhaps, England.

In Egypt, we grew the first commercial crop of broccoli which anybody in that country knew about. It was certainly the first the export officials had ever seen, causing us severe problems when they demanded we remove the stems like the cauliflower they were familiar with from the Nile Delta.

FORMS AVAILABLE

American broccoli varieties are far superior to those found through much of Europe. The varieties available to us here have larger, more compact heads and are more tender than the European varieties. Even our heavy stalks are still tender and can be eaten with pleasure.

BROCCOLI VARIETIES
Approximately 9,000 Seeds per Ounce, 34 Plants per 50 Feet

VARIETY*	DAYS TO MATURITY**	SPECIAL FEATURES
GREEN COMET HYBRID	55	Extra early, large head
GREEN DUKE HYBRID	70	Dome-shaped heads
CLEOPATRA HYBRID	55	Cold and drought resistant

*Hybrid broccoli is much preferred over open-pollinated types.
**Number of days from plants set in the garden.

PLANTING AND GROWING

Like beets, broccoli is one of the really superior plants for early spring here in the South. Start broccoli from seed in January inside or in a hot bed to have plants for setting outside as early in March as weather permits. You can also plant broccoli seed directly in the ground at the same time the plants are set for a later crop.

Grow broccoli in the spring and fall. The criterion is that it should mature in cool weather. I prefer growing broccoli on raised beds about 24 inches wide with 3 feet between the edges of the beds, which allows a tiller to cultivate between beds. After making the beds, fertilize with a 10-10-10 fertilizer on top of the beds. Open a furrow 4 to 6 inches deep for plants or 1 inch deep for seed. Set the plants in the row 18 inches apart, as soon as hard freezes have passed. For a fall crop, set plants in early September. Direct seeding in the spring should be done as quickly as the weather moderates. For a fall crop, plant seeds directly into the soil in August. Plant seeds about 1/4 to 1/2 inch deep. Thin the seedlings so that the plants are spaced 18 inches apart.

In gardens which cannot be watered or tend to be dry in the fall, it is better to use the furrow method of planting than the raised bed method. This will make it easier for the roots to seek subsurface moisture. Many gardeners are now using the double row system on each 24-inch bed. These rows should be 12 inches apart. By doubling the rows on the bed, you can use your space with greater efficiency.

The secret to good broccoli, however, is to be able to cut the heads while the weather is cool. If you plant later and harvest in hot weather, you get a lower quality broccoli and bring the plant into the cycle of the very destructive cabbage looper.

Ideally, the heads should be at their prime in late April and early May. After you cut the main heads, side-dress the crop with a 6-12-12 fertilizer to keep the plants healthy and to force more side shoots for continued harvest. You can continue to harvest them until the loopers arrive or hot weather causes the yellow flowers to open in the head.

Harvest broccoli while the "beads" are still tight. A few warm, sunny days will cause the flowers to open, and once any yellow appears, the quality goes down rapidly. The stalks of broccoli are fleshy and will quickly go through a heat if you do not handle them properly. Take the harvested head directly to a sink filled with ice and water. Immerse the heads and stems in the very cold water for 10 to 15 minutes, shake them dry, and refrigerate them immediately. This procedure takes the field heat out of the stems and will allow you to store the broccoli in the refrigerator for a much longer period of time. Broccoli also freezes extremely well, and you should freeze any you cannot eat within several days for later use.

Broccoli is an ideal fall crop to follow tomatoes or melons in the garden rotation.

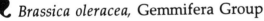 BRUSSELS SPROUT
Brassica oleracea, Gemmifera Group

HISTORY

Brussels sprouts are another member of the cabbage group but one not widely grown in the South. There are too many other members of the group which are more satisfactory. Brussels sprouts are a long-maturing crop and our climate is not really conducive to good production. Brussels sprouts need cool temperatures to develop properly, and because they are susceptible to the cabbage worm, it is hard to grow them in the summer without constant attention.

In Europe the small cabbages which form in the axiles of the leaves are a real delicacy, and are widely grown and used. In this country, however, they are not nearly so commonly grown and are rarely seen except in cooler climates. I have grown them with little success; the heat of our fall generally makes the sprouts tough. Spring plantings do not produce well either, because the long number of days to maturity brings harvest at a time when the weather is hot, making hard, tough sprouts.

FORMS AVAILABLE

I have grown only *Jade Cross* Hybrid, which is listed as 85 days from plants. *Prince Marvel* Hybrid has been reported as being somewhat superior, but 5 days longer (90 days) if maturing from plants.

PLANTING AND GROWING

Consider Brussels sprouts only for the fall garden. Start seeds in a seed bed or open cold frame during early July. Have the seedlings ready for setting in the garden in early August, and then keep them dusted or sprayed with both Sevin and Bacillus Thuringiensis to control aphids and cabbage worms.

Direct seeding is possible, though I prefer the controlled conditions of the seed bed to get a good start. In the garden, set or thin the plants to 18 inches apart in rows wide enough to cultivate frequently since growth of weeds and weed grasses is at a peak during the time of sprout production.

Plant Brussels sprouts in furrows opened in well-tilled soil. Make the furrow 6 inches deep and place 10-10-10 fertilizer in the bottom. When setting transplants, draw about 2 inches of soil into the furrow, mixing the fertilizer into the bottom of the furrow as you do. Leave the furrow open enough to accommodate the roots of the young plants. The plants should be set slightly deeper than they were growing in the seed bed. Direct seeding should be done in a similar way except the furrow is filled to 1/2 inch of the top. After seeding, cover lightly so that the seed are no more than 1/2 inch deep.

Keep Brussels sprouts growing rapidly by irrigating when they are dry and side-dressing with additional 10-10-10 fertilizer. The plant will develop with a tall, strong stalk. Remove the lower leaves constantly as the plant grows because the sprouts develop best in the axile when the leaves are removed.

Keep plants free from weeds and weed grasses, and from aphids and cabbage worms.

Remove the sprouts when they are about 1 inch in size. The best quality sprouts will occur about the time of the first frost, which makes them sweeter. Keep plants growing and producing as long as possible in the fall or until the first hard freezes kill them.

PROBLEMS

Grow Brussels sprouts in the South with caution and only if irrigation is possible. It is one of those extra crops which is rewarding but somewhat troublesome. Also beware of aphids and cabbage worms.

CABBAGE
Brassica oleracea, Capitata Group

HISTORY

It is difficult to think of a world without cabbage since it has been an important crop for so long. Cabbage comes from the wild cabbage still found in its rather ragged state on the coasts of England. It was known to the Greeks and widely grown by the Romans.

Evelyn describes it in 1683 as an important crop that had so many "sorts," one could not possibly grow all of them in the garden. White, in *Gardening for The South*, 1868, devotes nine pages to cabbage with descriptions of both plain and *Savoy* types. In his variety listing are some which are still grown today, like *Flat Dutch* and *Drumhead Savoy*.

FORMS AVAILABLE

Since the earlier maturing cabbages are generally the best for the home gardener, I always plant a portion of the crop with an open-pollinated variety. Hybrid cabbages are very uniform and tend to reach maturity at the same time, giving me more cabbage than I want to eat. The open-pollinated varieties are less uniform and can be harvested over a longer period of time. Use only very hardy varieties like *Early Jersey Wakefield* for overwintering.

CABBAGE VARIETIES
Set Plants 18 Inches Apart; 1 Ounce Has 9,000 Seeds

VARIETY	DAYS TO MATURITY**	SPECIAL FEATURES
COPENHAGEN MARKET	69	Early, round
EARLY FLAT DUTCH	70–80	Flat, round
EARLY JERSEY WAKEFIELD*	50	Conical shape
RED ACRE	75	Early, red
SAVOY KING HYBRID	90	Crinkled leaves
STONEHEAD HYBRID	50	Early, very solid

*Excellent for overwintering
**Number of days from plants set in the garden

PLANTING AND GROWING

In the South, cabbage is grown both as a spring and a fall crop, doing equally well in either season. I have also planted cabbage in October and overwintered the plants for an earlier spring crop, which attests to their hardiness. In fact, the range of its adaptation makes cabbage an extremely important crop. I have seen gorgeous cabbage grown in the Nile Delta of Egypt and also in Sweden. Few other crops of the garden can be grown over such a sizable area.

Prepare the garden well for growing cabbage and related plants. Deep tilling and addition of humus is very helpful. I prefer to grow the spring crop on beds and the fall crop in furrows made in very deeply-tilled garden areas. It is important to grow overwintering crops in furrows also to give the roots as much protection as possible. Take care never to plant cabbage in areas of the garden which tend to stay wet in the winter.

Start spring cabbage in cold frames, hotbeds, greenhouses, or cool, sunny areas inside the house at least six weeks ahead of anticipated setting time in the garden. Fall cabbage may be started in beds outside but should be watched for worm attacks and kept clean. Seed stores, nurseries, and plant shops are probably the best source of cabbage plants in the fall, but in the spring they seldom have new crop plants as early as I like to set them out.

Cabbage seedlings take from five to six weeks to develop into transplants stocky enough to stand early setting and sudden cold. In my area I like to set cabbage in the garden by March 10 in the spring and by September 10 in the fall.

After preparing the cabbage area, make wide beds 3 feet across and 3 feet apart. You can grow cabbages in 2 rows per bed with the rows 12 inches apart and

Red Acre Cabbage

Savoy King Cabbage

Stonehead Hybrid Cabbage

Plant cabbage early to mature
before the major worm infestations.

the plants 18 inches apart in the row. Stagger plants between the rows when planting. Make the furrows in the bed about 4 inches deep and apply 10-10-10 fertilizer to the bottom, working the fertilizer into the furrow with a pointed hoe. Set the cabbage plants so that they are covered up to the first leaves on the stem.

When the plants first start to form a head, side-dress them with 10-10-10 fertilizer to maximize the growth of the head.

I plant fall cabbage in a similar way, except I do not use the raised bed and seldom plant the double rows since weeds and weed grass are a big problem at this time, and cultivation between the two close rows is difficult. I make a 4-inch furrow in well-prepared soil with the furrows 3 feet apart for tilling purposes. Set the plants 18 inches apart in the row and follow the same fertilizing program used in the spring.

Cabbage may be set in the garden during early October for an overwintering crop. The plants will not survive a winter as intense as one in Michigan, but will come through quite well in a normal Southern year. It is certainly worth a try at setting an early spring crop.

PROBLEMS

Both spring and fall crops should be timed to reach the harvest stage before the cabbage worm (cabbage looper) arrives, or after it leaves. This insect is extremely destructive and can riddle the heads, making them useless. Very early spring plantings and plantings in early September usually reach the harvest stage when the worms are not active. You can control the worm by the use of some form of Bacillus Thuringiensis, a natural control which is very effective either as a dust or a spray. But timing is still the least expensive and most effective way of insuring worm-free crops.

Rotation is also advisable since there are root insects and diseases which may reduce yields. A three-year rotation is best, keeping any area free from all members of the cabbage family during that time. Contact the County Extension Service for the latest controls of root maggots, aphids, and the club-root disease.

❦ CHINESE CABBAGE
Brassica rapa

HISTORY

Chinese cabbage is relatively new to the western world, having come from China to Europe in the 19th century. Abercrombie fails to mention it in his book published in 1823, but Sturtevant reports its arrival in 1839. White fails to mention it in *Gardening for The South*, 1868. However, in the early 1900s it was listed in Southern seed catalogs. It is very much in demand in Europe but used very sparingly in this country. As Oriental dishes are served more and more, the delicious Chinese cabbage should become better known.

FORMS AVAILABLE

There are two types of this vegetable, *Pe-tsai* and *Pak-choi*. The main difference is in the shape. *Pe-tsai* is long and conical, with an almost celery-type stalk; the *Pak-choi* is more like cabbage with an oval head and a lesser stem.

Pe-tsai-type Chinese cabbage is usually referred to as *Michihili*. There is a new hybrid called *Michihili Jade Pagoda* Hybrid which is said to be earlier and should be more tender.

Pak-choi-type Chinese cabbage is often referred to as the *Napa* type. Commercial breeders are producing quite a few hybrid varieties which should be better than the old types. Some are said to be more heat-resistant. However, the long conical *Pe-tsai* types are in much more demand in Europe and are considered to be superior.

PLANTING AND GROWING

Chinese cabbage is frost-hardy but will not stand as much cold as cabbage. Plants should be set in cool weather, in the South about March 15. It takes about two months to grow a crop, so start as early as possible after hard freezes. Harvest the plants before hot weather for the best quality heads. I have never seen a fall crop in this country, but in Israel and Egypt it is grown frequently for the late European market and should do well in the South. I would suggest planting in mid to late August for the fall crop.

In Egypt we grew Chinese cabbage just like regular cabbage, on 3-foot beds with 2 rows per bed, staggering the plants. But we did it this way because all our machinery was set for that spacing. For the home garden you can reduce the spacing to 15 inches if set by hand.

Use the same fertilizers and fertilizing schedules as for cabbage.

Try Chinese cabbage. I believe you will adopt it as a regular crop.

 CARROT
Daucus Carota var. *sativus*

HISTORY

The carrot is found growing wild in Europe and the Middle East, though this form is certainly not the rich edible carrot with which we are familiar. It has always been widespread, being known in China during the 1200s. The edible form is said to have come to England during Queen Elizabeth's reign. Bailey, in *The Standard Cyclopedia of Horticulture*, testily states that the wild carrot is one of the bad weeds introduced into America. Certainly, any gardener will agree as they fight the scourge of this long-rooted, free-seeding pest. However, the great French seedsman Vilmorin is reported to have taken the wild carrot and in three generations selected the edible form.

None of this should detract from the rewards that the cultivated carrot brings to the garden. Everyone knows that carrots are good for the eyes, since they have the highest level of Vitamin A of any of the common vegetables with the exception of hot chili peppers. Evelyn describes carrot cultivation in detail in 1678, and Abercrombie gives it considerable attention in 1823. White lists four varieties in his *Gardening for The South* in 1868. Seed catalogs of the early 1900s had rather extensive listings.

FORMS AVAILABLE

Today, carrots may be usefully divided into five types based mainly on the shape of the root:

- The **Imperator** type has a small crown, and the root is long with a slim taper.
- The **Nantes** type has a medium-sized crown, and the root is long, coming to a blunt end.
- The **Chantenay** type has a large crown and the taper is severe.
- The **Round** type has roots that are almost round and are generally grown as forced or greenhouse/hotbed carrots
- The **Lady Finger** type is a tiny carrot that is either forced or grown in the field.

In addition to our standard carrot-colored types, the red carrots are gaining popularity, especially in Europe.

CARROT VARIETIES
½ Ounce Will Seed 50 Feet of Row

VARIETY	DAYS TO MATURITY	SPECIAL FEATURES
IMPERATOR TYPE		
Orlando Gold Hybrid	75–85	Deep orange
NANTES TYPE		
Nantes Scarlet	68	Small core
CHANTENAY TYPE		
Royal Chantenay	70	Large size, yet tender
LADY FINGER TYPE		
Lady Finger	65	Tiny, very sweet
Amstel	62	Small, good for hotbeds

PLANTING AND GROWING

Carrots are another of those excellent spring crops which can extend the harvest time of your garden. Seed them as early in the spring as the soil can be worked, or in mid-August for a fall crop which you can leave in the ground well into the winter and harvest as needed.

Carrots are slow to germinate. Because the seed are fine and the seedlings miniscule, it is essential that you keep the soil from crusting over. You need to cultivate lightly to keep the crust broken since it is extremely difficult to determine exactly where the row is. A simple solution is to plant a companion crop of Bibb lettuce or radishes in the row since these germinate quickly and will mark the row.

Carrots produce poorly in tight, sticky soil and are usually a disaster if planted in deep furrows. Use the raised bed method of planting in both spring and fall. To conserve space, make the bed at least 30 inches across in order to have two rows of carrots 12 to 15 inches apart. I make the space between the beds at least 3 feet to accommodate a tiller because continuous cultivation is absolutely necessary to control winter weeds and to keep the soil loose for good root development.

After preparing the soil and making the beds, fertilize with a 10-10-10 fertilizer and work it into the bed. About six weeks later, side-dress with a 6-12-12 fertilizer.

To plant, open a very shallow row and seed the combination of carrots and companion lettuce, covering the seed no more than 1/2 inch. When the carrots have germinated, thin them to a 3- to 4-inch spacing for the normal size varieties and remove the radish or lettuce companions. If you are using lettuce, you may carefully transplant it for development into a full crop.

Harvest the spring crop as soon as the exposed crown is of sufficient size. If you leave it too long, the roots will become less sweet and too fibrous. Harvest the fall crop as needed until the temperature of the soil goes below 20 degrees. During mild winters you may leave carrots in the ground until spring.

CAULIFLOWER
Brassica oleracea, Botrytis Group

HISTORY

Cauliflower is neither as tolerant to adverse weather or soil conditions, nor as easy to grow as cabbage or broccoli, but it is worth growing in the Southern garden. The new early hybrids have made a distinct difference in the ease of growth and cultivation.

Cauliflower is widely grown throughout much of the world. Beautiful heads are commonly seen in the fields of the Nile Delta in Egypt, unlike broccoli which is practically unheard of. On the continent of Europe cauliflower is still more popular than broccoli and much more widely grown. It evidently arrived in England in the 17th century; Abercrombie details its culture in 1823. By that time two varieties were listed merely as early and late, rather than by name.

FORMS AVAILABLE

Cauliflower is a type of cabbage in the same group as broccoli but with "curds" of white malformed flowers making the head.

CAULIFLOWER VARIETIES
9,000 Seed per Ounce

VARIETY	DAYS TO MATURITY*	SPECIAL FEATURES
SNOW KING HYBRID	50	Very early, heat-resistant
SNOWBALL X (EARLY SNOWBALL)	60	Large heads, self-blanching

*Days from setting transplants

Imperator type carrot; long and tapered

Snowball X Cauliflower

Fold leaves over to protect the head of cauliflower from the hot sun.

Green Pascal Celery

PLANTING AND GROWING

Cauliflower is temperamental and needs to be grown carefully by not subjecting it to heat or drought. The new early hybrids can be planted as soon as possible in the spring so that they will mature before the arrival of hot weather and the cabbage worm, which can devastate the head in an instant. However, cauliflower is less hardy than broccoli or cabbage and must be set after the hard freezes have passed. I have had the best success in planting in mid to late March. You can plant earlier if you provide a cover for the young transplants.

I have been successful only with spring cauliflower, though I have heard of success in the fall by gardeners who plant the first of September and keep the plants growing through our dry Octobers with some type of irrigation.

Start cauliflower seeds inside or in a greenhouse, hot bed, or cold frame. I seed in a tray, transplanting to a 2¼-inch pot as soon as the true leaves have formed and the plants are strong enough to be handled. Grow these small plants in a cool bright place like a cold frame to keep them from becoming leggy.

The cultivation of cauliflower is virtually the same as for broccoli and cabbage up until the first appearance of the heads. At this time I carefully pull the top leaves over the head and staple them together with a toothpick or small twig. This treatment will help to keep the head white and prevent the hot sun from browning the curds or causing quick opening of the flowers which ruins the head as an edible dish.

Cut the heads as soon as they are fully developed, while the curds are still tight. Since the flower stalks will "run up" quickly on hot days, you must watch the harvesting carefully. Cold-treat the heads as described for broccoli to insure longer life in the refrigerator.

PROBLEMS

If the cauliflower matures late, the cabbage worm becomes a real problem. Its best control is early planting, though Bacillus Thuringiensis is excellent if applied as the first worms arrive. There is nothing more appalling than to find great numbers of worms deeply embedded in the beautiful curds when you wash them.

CELERIAC
Apium graveolens var. *rapaceum*

Celeriac is grown for the fleshy root rather than the leaf stalk. It is somewhat less known than celery but is easier to grow and produces under less strict conditions. Grow celeriac the same way as celery except set the plants at ground level in the furrow. No blanching is required, and the useful portion is the bulbous, swollen crown which is cooked and has the taste of celery. The leafy portion is useless.

Celeriac is used primarily for cooking to achieve the flavor of celery. It is also boiled and eaten or made into celery soup.

Celeriac is grown in exactly the same manner as celery. The only difference in these two plants is that celeriac is grown for the crown which has the taste of celery. The leafy shoots are discarded. Blanching is, also, not necessary.

Large Smooth Prague is a variety which takes 110 days to mature.

☘ CELERY
Apium graveolens var. *dulce*

HISTORY

Neither celery nor its cousin, celeriac (*Apium graveolens* var. *rapaceum*), can be considered ideal plants for the Southern garden. Their season for maturing is very long, almost four months, and they are among the few crops which are generally far superior when grown commercially as opposed to cultivating in the home garden. American commercial celery production is highly efficient and the cost to the consumer is low.

FORMS AVAILABLE

Green Pascal is the celery commonly grown in this country. There are now some hybrids of this type that may be more uniform, but *Green Pascal* is certainly the most widely-adapted variety for gardens. It is resistant to blight which can be a serious problem.

CELERY VARIETIES
72,000 Seed per Ounce

VARIETY	DAYS TO MATURITY*	SPECIAL FEATURES
GREEN PASCAL	120	Blight-resistant
CELERIAC	110	Grown for crowns

*Days are from sprouted seedlings. Starting inside will reduce field time by about one month.

PLANTING AND GROWING

Only the most industrious gardener should attempt to grow this plant. During its entire season, it needs good, rich, high-humus soil which holds moisture during dry periods but is not wet during heavy rain. The best way to grow celery is in beds made with heavy timbers or cross ties and filled with rich, well-drained soil.

Celery should be planted as early in the spring as the ground can be safely worked. Since the seeds are slow to germinate, start them in early January in frames or in a sunny place. Sow them in cells, several seeds in each, so that you will not need to transplant them from a seed flat into pots. After the seeds have germinated and the young plants are thriving, set the trays of cells outside on cool days when the sun is shining to harden them and to keep the young plants stocky. Keep them away from frost or freezing weather at this time, but do not let them become spindly and succulent.

Celery does well when it follows crimson clover in the rotation. Work the soil for celery beds as deeply as possible and turn under liberal amounts of humus. Make a 6-inch furrow and fertilize with a 6-12-12 fertilizer, working it into the furrow and drawing loose soil in slightly. Set the young plants 12 inches apart in the row and make the rows far enough apart to cultivate with a tiller. If planting in raised beds, the rows may be as close as 2 feet apart. Plant the celery from the cell packs deep in the furrow so that soil may be drawn against the stem as the plant develops. Six weeks after planting when the plants are 12 inches high, side-dress lightly with ammonium nitrate to encourage rapid growth.

Keep celery evenly moist! The most destructive growth problem is dry soil during the development of the stalks. May is usually our second driest month, and celery must be irrigated then.

Celery is ready to cut when the stalks are strong and spread widely at the base. The plant will reach a maximum of about two feet at maturity. After cutting, cool the bunches in ice water to take out the field heat. Refrigerate immediately to give the celery a long use period.

Though Americans generally do not blanch celery, the 12-inch spacing will help to blanch the lower stems somewhat. If you want to blanch celery, the easiest way in the garden is to obtain some 6-inch terra cotta pipes which have been cut to 15-inch lengths and slip these over the developing plants so that the tops will show.

 SWISS CHARD
Beta vulgaris, Cicla Group

HISTORY

This bottomless beet-type plant is a great substitute for spinach during the late spring and early summer. Swiss chard is grown like beets except that it is not absolutely necessary to grow it in beds since no bulbous root is forming.

FORMS AVAILABLE

SWISS CHARD VARIETIES
Sow 1 Ounce per 50 Feet of Row

VARIETY	DAYS TO MATURITY	SPECIAL FEATURES
LUCULLUS	55	Light green
RHUBARB	55	Red ribs

PLANTING AND GROWING

Planting starts when the first beets are sown and can continue until April for later crops. Swiss chard may also be grown as a fall crop like beets. The ribs may become tough and stringy as the summer heat comes, but I solve this by cutting the ribs out and boiling only the greens.

The secret of good chard production is to grow it quickly with high nitrogen fertilizers after the initial 10-10-10 is exhausted. I have found the very high nitrogen lawn fertilizers to be excellent as side-dressing after about six weeks of growth. Use these lightly, however, if the nitrogen is not a slow release variety.

The best way to harvest chard is to remove the outer leaves on a regular basis. This keeps new growth coming over a long period of time.

🌱 COLLARD
Brassica oleracea, Acephala Group

HISTORY

Collard greens and grits are as typically Southern as any two foods I know. The collard has a large amount of vitamin A and C and a terrible smell when cooking. It is not, as you can tell, one of my favorite dishes, but I shouldn't be so prejudiced because collards are easy to grow and contain much nutrition.

Botanically the collard is one of the "headless" cabbages, and it is not uncommon for writers of old to refer, as Sturtevant did, to early cabbages being grown as collards which to a Southerner is plain blasphemy. The collard is probably a form of kale which has similar characteristics but a different taste. Though White in *Gardening for The South* does not mention the collard, it was in Southern seed catalogs in the early 1900s, listed as Southern or Georgia Collards.

FORMS AVAILABLE

There are some hybrid collards now listed in seed catalogs. It is claimed that they are more compact and of better flavor. You may wish to try a few in your garden.

COLLARD VARIETIES
9,000 Seed per Ounce, Direct Seed ½ Ounce per 50 Ft. Row

VARIETY	DAYS TO MATURITY*	SPECIAL FEATURES
GEORGIA	70–75	Tall growing, compact
VATES	75	plant, very hardy
		for overwintering

*Days from setting transplants

PLANTING AND GROWING

Because collards will grow in poorer soil than cabbage will, it is a useful substitute when the ground is not good. The collard grows from 3 to 4 feet in height and forms a rosette of leaves which you may harvest a few at a time. It is a cool-weather crop, best planted with the early cabbages in the spring and in early to mid-August in the fall. Real collard lovers rate the fall crop as superior because the rosette of leaves mature near the first frost which makes them sweet and tender. I have often allowed the fall crop to remain in the garden over the winter to be cut back in early spring for a quick crop.

Grow collards in the same manner as all the cabbage group. The best way is in raised beds in the spring and furrows in the fall. My only other admonition is to keep collards heavy of leaf and growing rapidly by using a high nitrogen fertilizer about midway in the plant's development.

Lucullus Swiss Chard

Rhubarb Swiss Chard

Vates Collards

Silver Queen Sweet Corn

Corn stalk borer

Corn ear worm

Plant sweet corn in blocks of at least two rows.

♈ SWEET CORN
♌ Zea Mays var. *rugosa*

HISTORY

Corn is definitely an American plant. It was described in the *Popil Vuh*, the sacred book of the Quiche Indians of western Guatemala. Columbus found corn on his first expedition in 1492; the colonial settlers were given corn by the Indians and explorers found corn being grown by the Indians throughout the continent.

Sweet corn was introduced much later into the life of the colonists. Sturtevant states that this form of corn was first introduced to the Plymouth, Massachusetts area by a man with General Sullivan's expedition who received seeds from the Susquehanna Indians in 1779. Sweet corn was certainly not widely grown until the 19th century.

FORMS AVAILABLE

In the South, sweet corn is of much later acceptance. When I was young, we grew only a few test trials since the varieties on the market were singularly unsuited to the vagaries of Southern summers. My grandfather listed, however, three true sweet corn varieties in his 1909 catalog, including *Country Gentleman*, which was widely used even in the 1930s. Our table corn was always *Hastings' Prolific*, harvested in the roasting ear or milk stage.

Sweet corn, as a widely-grown Southern home garden plant, never came into its own until the variety *Silver Queen* was introduced. My country neighbors were still growing *Hastings' Prolific* as a table corn when we moved to our country place in 1968. After my first crop was spread around the neighborhood, *Silver Queen* became the favored variety. Each year I try some new variety but have never been convinced that any can equal *Silver Queen*'s ability to produce the highest quality sweet corn for the South, year in and year out, under every type of summer condition.

SWEET CORN VARIETIES
¼ lb. Will Seed 50 Feet of Row

VARIETY	COLOR	NUMBER OF DAYS	SPECIAL FEATURES
SILVER QUEEN*	White	88	Very strong plants, very sweet
GOLDEN QUEEN*	Yellow	88	Like Silver Queen
MERIT*	Yellow	80	Disease-resistant
STARDUST	White	70	Early
EARLY SUNGLOW	Yellow	62	Very early

*I consider these best for Southern gardens.

PLANTING AND GROWING

Success in growing sweet corn comes with careful timing, ample fertilizing, and clean cultivation. Sow the seed as quickly after frost as the ground begins to warm; the earlier you sow the better, since the sweetest kernels are made in periods of ample moisture before hot nights are common. Later plantings are always very susceptible to heavy attacks of the corn earworm and stalk borer, which will devastate the crop if left unchecked.

Since sweet corn has a concentrated harvest time, it is a good practice to divide the sweet corn area into three or four plots of two rows each (for good pollination) and to make plantings about two weeks apart, the last planting occurring the middle week of May. This will put the last harvest at the end of July when earworms are sparse enough to be controlled with careful use of Sevin and Bacillus Thuringiensis.

Sweet corn should be planted in blocks of at least two rows to give good pollen spread and complete pollination of the silks. Single row plantings may produce ears with many kernel skips and thus imperfect formation.

I plant the earliest blocks on beds which are 2 feet across and 12 inches deep to keep the seed, which has a tendency to rot in cold wet ground, out of a "water furrow." After the ground is warm, you can make later plantings in a furrow drawn through well-prepared soil. Be sure there is at least 3 feet between the edges of the beds so that you will not cut the side roots when using a tiller as a cultivator. If you do cut them, you will stunt the plants, prevent strong development, and cause poor formation of the ears.

I plant sweet corn in a drill, spacing the seed 2 to 3 inches apart, and thinning to 12 inches for the final spacing. Many gardeners still drop four or five seeds every 12 inches, and this is perfectly acceptable, though I find thinning easier if seeds are drilled. Plant seeds 1 inch deep.

Sweet corn is a gross feeder; it needs heavy fertilizing to produce good crops. I use a pre-plant application of a 10-10-10 fertilizer in the row and cover it lightly before seeding. Use additional nitrogen fertilizer as a side-dressing when the corn is knee-high. I find ammonium nitrate excellent for this application.

Clean cultivation is essential to good corn production. Kill any weeds and keep the soil loose, never allowing it to crust over for long periods of time. Since corn needs a lot of moisture, every bit of rainfall must be absorbed for the use of the plant and not be allowed to run off crusted soil.

Many gardeners consider, as I do, that sweet corn is the ultimate home garden crop. Sweet corn loses a tremendous amount of sugar within twenty-four hours of harvest, making it a home garden crop unequalled by any you can purchase fresh, frozen, or canned. The tastiest sweet corn to be eaten is that which you pull from your garden, take directly to the kitchen, and cook immediately.

Sweet corn does take space to produce, but it is well worth adding some area to your vegetable garden in order to grow it for the table.

PROBLEMS

Many insects and some diseases will attack sweet corn. The earworm and stalk borer are most destructive. When you notice them, deal with them promptly with a spray or dust of Sevin and Bacillus Thuringiensis (which may be obtained in a mixture). Japanese beetles may also be very destructive; they attack not only the foliage, but also the silks. Give prompt attention to the control of this pest because damage to the silks may prevent pollination and cause skips in the rows of kernels.

Sevin is an excellent beetle control and the mixture with the Bacillus will give good general results for a number of pests.

There are some diseases of corn which may be troublesome, especially smut. If these do occur, get the latest control recommendations from the County Extension Service in your area.

 POPCORN
Zea Mays var. *praecox*

HISTORY

Popcorn has always been considered a novelty for the garden, but you should consider it as a useful crop if you have available space. Take care to plant popcorn away from sweet corn to prevent cross-pollination which will increase the starch content of the sweet corn.

FORMS AVAILABLE

Most varieties will take three and one-half months to be ready. Hybrid varieties like *White Cloud* and *South American Hybrid* are generally best for the home garden.

PLANTING AND GROWING

Grow popcorn exactly like sweet corn, using the same methods, except that you do not need successive plantings. Plant as soon as the danger of frost has passed. Since the kernels have more starch, plant the early crops in furrows rather than beds to increase resistance to rotting.

Allow popcorn to mature completely, however, and do not pull until the shucks are dry and tan. After pulling, hang them or lay them in a cool dry place for several weeks to a month. Shell the kernels from the cob and store them in closed jars in a cool place.

 CUCUMBER
Cucumis sativus

HISTORY

The cucumber is one of the oldest cultivated plants in the world. According to Sturtevant, it probably originated in the East Indies and was carried to Egypt 3,000 years ago. Cucumbers were grown in the early 14th century in England and were said to have been cultivated by Columbus in the West Indies in 1494.

They have been an important part of American gardens from their beginning. White describes their cultivation in detail and lists five varieties suitable to Southern cultivation. My grandfather listed nine varieties in 1909, including the *Japanese Climbing Cucumber* for trellises.

FORMS AVAILABLE

Today the cucumber is grown almost universally in Southern gardens. With the development of the dwarf bush varieties, it can be grown in any small area, even in pots.

The difference between slicing and pickling cucumbers is now mainly a difference in the "blockiness" of the fruit rather than the color of the spines, black for pickling and white for slicing. Pickling varieties have fruit with a length-diameter ratio of 3 to 1, while slicing varieties are generally 4 to 1.

The greatest addition to the cucumber world has been the "burpless" varieties which are quite long, have extremely small seed cavities, and few seeds. These will remain crisp and tender when left much longer on the vine than older varieties. They are also distinctly lacking in the aftertaste of most other cucumbers.

The botany of the cucumber is important to understand. The flower sexes are separate, usually on the same vine. It is common for gardeners to become concerned about the lack of fruit set from early flowers. This is due to the fact that the earliest flowers, which are male, precede the female flowers by a week or more. Patience is all that is needed. Soon the female flowers appear and fruit set begins. Both male and female flowers continue to blossom as long as the plant is actively growing. A number of new varieties have been developed with only female flowers. A variety with both is always added to the package, but using these gynoecious varieties may cause problems if all the pollinator varieties are thinned out or perhaps not planted. The home gardener should always stick to the monoecious varieties (male and female flowers).

There are a number of "bush" and pot varieties which have been introduced for restricted places. Of these varieties, I have grown only *Pot Luck*, which was satisfactory for the purpose but certainly was not in a class with the following varieties.

CUCUMBER VARIETIES
⅛ Ounce per 50 Feet of Row, 1,000 Seeds per Ounce

VARIETY	DAYS	RESISTANCE*	SPECIAL FEATURES
SWEET SLICE HYBRID	63	1,2,3,4	Burpless type
POINSETT 76	63	1,2,5,6,7	Very disease-resistant
SWEET SUCCESS HYBRID	54	3,5,8	Seedless, very mild
LIBERTY HYBRID	54	2,5,6	Pickling
SUMTER	56	1,2,3,5,6,7	Disease-resistant

*Resistance: 1. Powdery Mildew   5. Cucumber Scab
2. Downy Mildew   6. Angular Leaf Spot
3. Cucumber Mosaic Virus   7. Anthracnose
4. Watermelon Mosaic Virus   8. Target Leaf Spot

PLANTING AND GROWING

Grow cucumbers during warm weather. Planting too early may cause the seed to germinate poorly or, if germination occurs, the vines to grow weakly. Plant after the danger of frost when the ground begins to warm. Growing cucumbers is equally satisfactory in hills or in beds. By planting in beds, out of the water furrow, in the early spring, there is less chance that seeds will rot.

Modern hybrid cucumbers are firm and tender with small seeds even when the fruits are large.

Downy mildew on cucumbers

Poinsett Cucumber

Cucumbers grown on strings stretched between bamboo poles set in the row.

Sweet Slice cucumber is very mild.

Cucumbers grown on a heavy bamboo structure

Flea beetles on eggplant set out too early

Dusky Hybrid Eggplant

Though the usual practice is to grow cucumbers on the ground, they take a lot of space and the rows must be at least 3 or 4 feet apart. A space-saving way is to grow them on trellises, wires, or fences. I set a 6-foot long, 3-inch post at each end of a 15-foot row and run a No. 10 wire between the two at the top and another wire two feet off the ground. Then I either run strings from the top wire to the bottom wire for the vines to climb, or fasten a heavy nylon mesh cloth between the two wires for the tendrils to grasp.

Plant three to five seeds per hill and make hills 3 feet apart, or sow in a shallow furrow if you use a bed. Plants grown on a bed should be spaced 12 inches apart. When planting on a bed I usually put two seeds every foot and remove the weaker one later. You should thin hill plantings to the two best vines.

Use a 10-10-10 pre-plant fertilizer and apply a 6-12-12 or a 5-10-15 fertilizer about every six weeks thereafter.

Keep fruits picked regularly. Leaving fruits on the vine reduces the future harvest!

PROBLEMS

Cucumbers are attacked by a number of beetles, especially the striped or the spotted cucumber beetle. Give extreme care to the germinating seedlings, because these beetles can ruin the young plants almost overnight. Dust the emerging plants regularly with Sevin to control them. There are a number of other insects and diseases which attack cucumbers. Fortunately, many new varieties are resistant to mosaic and to the mildews, which reduces considerably the need for dusting and spraying. Check with the County Extension Service in your area for control of specific problems.

EGGPLANT
Solanum Melongena

HISTORY

The eggplant or aubergine (the European name) is typically a Southern plant, being happiest in hot weather. It is strictly a summer vegetable, and even in Egypt the crops were finished by late November.

Its origins are not exactly known, but the supposition is that it came from the tropical East Indies via the Middle East to Europe in the 15th century. Evelyn doesn't mention it in his 16th-century treatise. Abercrombie lists it as an ornamental in 1823 but not as a vegetable. White gives detailed instructions as to its culture, listing three varieties in 1868. My grandfather had two varieties in his 1909 catalog, one of which was listed earlier by White. Today this vegetable is popular throughout much of the world and is relished in Europe and the Middle East. Japanese seedsmen are trying to improve the varieties, especially in the development of the long slender types popular in the Orient and in Europe.

Eggplant is an attractive plant which I have seen grown in ornamental gardens for beauty and fruit. Since a few fruits go a long way on the table, five or six plants will provide most that a family might need. So growing eggplant in a large border with flowers has much appeal.

FORMS AVAILABLE

The popular eggplant for Southern gardens is the one with large oval-shaped fruit produced on rather bushy dwarf plants. The tall-growing older types we saw in the Nile Delta which were formerly popular in the United States are too big and cumbersome for most of our modern gardens.

EGGPLANT VARIETIES
6,000 Seeds per Ounce

VARIETY	DAYS TO MATURITY*	SPECIAL FEATURES
BEAUTY HYBRID	66	Large, oval purple fruit
DUSKY HYBRID	63	Very dark purple fruit
BLACK BEAUTY	82	Large bush and large fruit
ICHIBAN HYBRID	58	Large bush and long slim fruit

*From plants

PLANTING AND GROWING

I grow eggplant in a short row in the vegetable garden, finishing the row with hot peppers, another crop which produces a gracious plenty from a few plants.

Two important features of eggplant determine the way they are to be grown. First, they are susceptible to verticillium wilt, which is also a problem on tomatoes and sweet peppers. Eggplant should therefore never be grown in an area of the garden where these other two crops have been planted previously within three or four years. Second, eggplant is a hot-weather plant which should not be set in the garden until the night temperatures reach the 60s. The plants not only grow poorly in cool temperatures; they are also riddled with the flea beetle until the weather gets warm. Early setting of the plants does very little to hasten the harvest anyway since they just sit there growing slowly until the temperatures are right.

Start seeds inside when you start tomatoes and peppers because eggplant takes longer to develop in trays or pots than the other vegetables do.

I grow eggplant about 24 inches apart with 3 feet between each bed. I usually plant them in relatively dry areas since they withstand drought conditions well. Apply 10-10-10 to the bed as a pre-plant fertilizer. When growth becomes vigorous and you see the first blooms, fertilize again with a 6-12-12 or 5-10-15 formula. Keep plants growing rapidly throughout their bearing season.

If flea beetles persist, keep the plants thoroughly dusted or sprayed, especially on the undersides of the leaves, with Malathion and Diazinon.

Harvest fruits when they have colored well and have reached a good size. Since the fruits will stand on the plant for some length of time, you may harvest as you need them.

The secret of eggplant production is proper timing, clean soil, good growth, and constant cultivation or mulching to keep free from weeds.

PROBLEMS

Control flea beetles by dusting or spraying the undersides of leaves with Malathion or mulching to keep free from weeds.

ENDIVE
Cichorium Endivia

Endive is used as a lettuce substitute during times when lettuce is unavailable. In some areas it is relished as a salad green. It is best grown in cool weather, which makes the spring crop difficult in the South because of its three-month maturity time. Plant in the earliest part of August for a fall crop.

Grow endive in well-prepared garden soil which you have fertilized with a 10-10-10 fertilizer. Sow seeds in drills at the rate of 1/2 ounce per 50 feet of row and cover with only 1/2 inch of soil. Keep growing rapidly with additional fertilizer as needed. Irrigate when conditions are dry. Harvest endive in late October and early November, or earlier if it has reached suitable size.

ESCAROLE
Cichorium Endivia

Escarole is a type of endive with broader, flat leaves. Its culture is the same as for endive.

GOURDS
Cucurbita, Lagenaria, Luffa, and other genera

You may grow many types and varieties of gourds in the summer garden. Since some take many, many days to mature, they should be planted as soon as the ground warms in the spring. You can see bird house, dipper, dish rag (Luffa), ornamental, and many other kinds of gourds at garden supply outlets.

Most gourds are long vine plants and do best when grown on some type of support like a fence, wire, or trellis. I plant gourds on a 2-wire fence in hills to allow earlier planting. Use 10-10-10 as a pre-plant fertilizer, but switch to a 6-12-12 during the growing season. I mulch the plants heavily to lessen the need for constant cultivation and weed control.

Since gourds have few problems, spraying is unnecessary unless you see some specific insect. Some varieties are susceptible to mildew, but it seldom disturbs the production. If mildew does seem to be an impediment to production, use the same type sprays you use for squash and cucumbers.

Harvest gourds when they mature and have lost all their green color and have turned tan, except in the case of ornamental gourds, which can be removed while still brightly-colored. Bird house gourds should remain on the vine until the skin has turned a light tan, and the insides are dry enough to be easily removed by shaking.

Luffas need a structure like this one made from bamboo at our project in the Philippines.

Filipinos find the Luffa better than a sandstone which is commonly used to scrub with.

Luffa, the fabulous sponge or dish-rag gourd

Kohlrabi

63

🌱 HORSERADISH
🍷 *Armoracia rusticana*

HISTORY

Horseradish is a crop like Jerusalem artichoke which grows easily and is a useful adjunct to any Southern garden. In this case, however, a little goes a long way, as does the sauce derived from the roots.

The plant is found wild in Europe and has been cultivated since the Middle Ages. In 1675 Evelyn called it a "gross" food eaten by the poor near Limoges, France. He writes of its use ". . . among the poorer people who diversly accommodate them, by boyling, frying, and eating them with Oyle, having first cut them in slices, and soake them in water to take away their rankness." In 1834, Abercrombie noted that horseradish was a common garden plant in England used, as we do, in a sauce. White gives detailed instructions for its culture in the South, indicating its wide use here in 1868.

Its use now is primarily for horseradish sauce which is made from shredded roots. Real, freshly-made horseradish sauce bears little resemblance to the creamy glop served in small packages at fast food restaurants. The best I have ever tasted was the product of a Mr. Cefalu, who owned a small market in mid-town Atlanta. This freshly-prepared sauce made a roast beef dinner a sublime experience. Since Mr. Cefalu's death there has been no more sauce and Atlantans are obliged to endure the regular market kinds. The only alternative for us all is to grow it ourselves and prepare our own sauce. Fortunately, that is not a difficult chore.

FORMS AVAILABLE

Horseradish seeds are not produced in sufficient quantities to make seeding a viable approach, so use root cuttings, which may be purchased in the spring. They usually come as bundles of straight pencil-sized roots which have been cut into 6-inch lengths.

PLANTING AND GROWING

Grow horseradish in the same type of soil and beds which you prepare for Jerusalem artichokes. Fertilize the bed with a 10-10-10 and draw out a deep furrow in the center. Plant any time after the hardest of freezing temperatures has passed, usually in early March in the South.

Plant each root piece on a slant with the topmost point about 4 inches underground. Space the roots 18 inches apart in the row. The younger, straighter roots are the most desirable for kitchen use. Grow plants cleanly and rapidly, using one or two light side-dressings of a 6-12-12 fertilizer during the summer.

Harvest in the fall, just before the first very hard freezes occur. Since the best growth comes in the cool of the fall, leave in the ground as long as possible or until the tops are killed. Then dig up the entire plants and take up the roots. Separate the roots, saving the fleshiest and tenderest ones for the kitchen. At the same time, choose the number of roots you wish to reset for next year's plantings and cut them into 6-inch lengths. They should be long and straight like the ones you first purchased, between pencil size and 1/4 inch in diameter.

Ideally, horseradish for later use and for next spring's plantings should be stored in a root cellar or pit. However, few of us have these nowadays, so your second best choice is a cool cellar that is not too dry. You can bury the root stock for next year's plantings in very loamy soil in the garden, but never leave it buried in soil which is soggy or where water stands for even a short length of time.

Though horseradish may be left in the ground in a Southern winter and harvested as needed, this involves some risk. Since extreme cold may damage the roots, take care to remove all old roots from the ground. This plant, like the Jerusalem artichoke, can become a pest unless kept under control. It is ideal to remove all the plants in the fall and then till the garden in the early spring to rid the area of any old stock.

KALE
Brassica Napus, Pabularia Group

Dwarf Scotch kale is the type most widely grown in Southern gardens, and is planted for both a spring and fall crop. Kale is somewhat more hardy than collards, though both will stand heavy frosts and light freezes.

Grow kale the same way as collards and cabbage (see those sections for detailed cultural information), though you can plant it a little earlier in the spring to provide a quicker crop. You can also plant kale during late August and early September from transplants, or seed it directly in the garden in early August.

Set plants 14 inches apart in the row or thin them to that spacing.

Harvest kale by letting the whole plant reach a good size and taking all of it, or by removing the right number of leaves for one meal and leaving the plant to produce more.

The insect and disease problems of kale are similar to those of cabbage.

KOHLRABI
Brassica oleracea, Gongylodes Group

Kohlrabi is often referred to as stem turnip because the swollen stem is reminiscent of that plant. The edible part is the swollen stem, which is two to three inches in diameter and has somewhat the taste of a turnip.

These fast-maturing plants produce the edible portion in about 45 days after transplanting into the garden.

Springtime is the most common time to grow kohlrabi in the South. I start seed at the same time as cabbage and broccoli so that the plants are ready to set in the garden as soon as the hard freezes have passed. You can have a fall crop if you plant in late September. Because the best kohlrabi is grown rapidly in cool weather, plantings in August or early September often produce tough and bitter stems. If you irrigate fall crops in dry weather, the taste will be good. See cabbage culture for details of growing kohlrabi and for insect and disease problems.

Harvest kohlrabi when the swollen stem is 2 to 3 inches in diameter; larger stems become tough. You can eat kohlrabi raw with a dip or cook it like turnips.

 LETTUCE
Lactuca sativa

HISTORY

This epitome of salad plants is probably as old as the art of gardening itself. Its origin is thought to be the Orient though there are close relatives native to Europe. It was served to the Persian kings as noted by Herodotus, and all my ancient references give special note to its culture. In the early days of his company, my grandfather placed special emphasis upon lettuce, especially on the careful selection of seed, a practice of absolute necessity even today. Our farm manager in Egypt, John Huyck, demanded not only the best varieties but the best strains, and he held absolute allegiance to a certain group of seed producers in California, asserting that disaster would befall us if the highest quality of seed was not used.

FORMS AVAILABLE

There are three distinct types of lettuce commonly grown in the Southern garden. The first, and most common, is the loose leaf or butterhead type; the second is the cabbage head, more commonly called the Iceberg type; the third is the Cos or Romaine type which has a long, upright stalk. The term Iceberg lettuce may be a bit

LETTUCE VARIETIES
25,000 Seed per Ounce

VARIETY	DAYS TO MATURITY*	SPECIAL FEATURES
ICEBERG TYPE		
Great Lakes	75	Very solid heads
Vanguard	90	Heat-resistant
COS TYPE		
Parris Island Cos	70	Good green
BUTTERHEAD TYPE		
Kentucky Bibb	57	Small, compact
Buttercrunch	65	Large Bibb
Summer Bibb	60	Heat-tolerant
LOOSE LEAF TYPE		
Salad Bowl	45	Very early
Black-Seeded Simpson	45	Very hardy
Red Head	50	Red heads
Grand Rapids	43	Wavy leaves

*Days to maturity may vary according to the season; therefore use this only as a guide.

Salad Bowl Lettuce

Kentucky Bibb Lettuce

Red Head Lettuce

Vanguard Lettuce

Buttercrunch Lettuce

Planting lettuce by pressing the edge of a board into loose soil

Lettuce seed are carefully planted very shallowly. They will not germinate if covered too deeply.

confusing since *Iceberg* is a variety introduced many years ago that was listed by my grandfather in 1909. However, the name now commonly refers to the very tight cabbage head lettuces produced so unerringly in massive quantities in California.

The loose leaf or butterhead type is the most commonly grown of the garden lettuces because it is less temperamental and is extremely fast in maturing. The Iceberg type is much longer maturing and much less tolerant of weather and soil conditions. The Cos type lettuce will stand hotter weather and thus has a useful place in our gardens, but is most often overlooked and seldom used. This Cos type does not have the quality of Iceberg or loose leaf types, and is usually eliminated from garden plans because of the almost unending supply of high quality Iceberg lettuce in the market.

When you purchase lettuce seed, be sure you know something about the varieties. I prefer the Bibb lettuces for most of my plantings. These include such varieties as *Buttercrunch* and *Summer Bibb* as well as the common *Kentucky Bibb* lettuce. You should be aware of the distinction which many seedsmen make between the butterhead and the loose leaf lettuces. The butterhead makes a tighter rosette of leaves but not a true head; the loose leaf lettuces have little rosette form. The best varieties are *Salad Bowl, Red Head, Black-Seeded Simpson* (the most cold-hardy lettuce I have grown), and *Grand Rapids*. The best Cos or Romaine lettuce for the South is *Parris Island Cos,* which has a good green color. The cabbage head lettuces should be chosen carefully from those varieties which mature quickly in 70 to 75 days. The best three-month variety for the South is *Vanguard,* which is very heat tolerant, but be careful not to allow it to dry out.

PLANTING AND GROWING

Lettuce is a hardy annual which does best when planted as soon as possible after the severest freezes have passed. Many of the loose leaf types mature in less than fifty days, and so a succession of plantings is advisable. The common procedure is to plant all lettuce so that the final harvest is taken before the hottest of weather has arrived. Lettuce has a tendency to become bitter, to bolt, and to go to seed during hot weather. However, a very fine gardener I know, Madame Coldelet, grows Bibb lettuce throughout the hot summers of Northern Morocco by planting it on the south side of very high beds prepared between orange and lemon plants in her garden. This gives ample sunlight in the morning and afternoon but protects the plants from the hot mid-day sun. Each time I visited the Coldelets, I was treated to Madame's incredible fresh salads made from her home-grown lettuce, no matter what season I was there. She told me that her summer success was due entirely to frequent irrigation and this mid-day shading. This practice should be applicable to us in the South, provided we use the raised beds and frequent furrow irrigation as well as the shade.

Lettuce requires rich, loose soil and excellent drainage. Heavy clay soil must be amended with ample humus or ground bark, and raised beds should be used for growing the crop.

Prepare the ground for lettuce as early as possible, usually at the same time you prepare the areas for cabbage and other early hardy vegetables. Raise your lettuce beds at least 12 inches above the furrow and make them 20 to 24 inches across or with enough room for two rows 12 inches apart on the bed. Plant 6 feet of row at a time to yield enough lettuce for a family of four or five.

I start lettuce in three different ways each year which, when taken together, gives me a continuous supply. First, I start seed in seed trays in mid-January, transplanting to cells or small 2¼-inch pots as soon as they are tough, and the true leaves have started forming. I set them in the garden as soon as the weather moderates and the danger of hard freezes has passed. Second, at that same time, I sow lettuce seed rather thickly in one of the two rows on the bed. Third, when these seeds have reached the thinning stage, I transplant the thinnings to the second row on the bed. By two weeks into the growing season in the garden, I have lettuce in three different stages of growth, which spreads the harvest from one general planting time. Then I make several more seedings in other beds, using the same thinning and transplanting method, and that gives me good lettuce until hot weather.

The butterhead type should be spaced 6 inches apart and the Iceberg type spaced 12 inches apart in the row. Cos lettuce is planted like the butterhead type.

Plant lettuce seed carefully, whether in trays or in the open ground. *Caution:* If lettuce seeds are covered too deeply, they will not germinate properly. Open the furrow with a pointed hoe, barely making a mark in the soil. Drop seeds rather thickly and draw a very light layer of loose soil over the seed. Since the seed should not dry out after seeding, you should water them very lightly if the soil becomes dry. How you handle the seeds prior to planting is also important. Seed purchased in packages at a store should be kept cool (below 65 degrees) and should not be placed where the humidity is high, as in a greenhouse. The combination of high humidity and high temperature will quickly kill the germination of the seed.

The secret to good production is rapid growth and plenty of water. This is not usually a problem during the first two months of production (mid-March to mid-May) because our natural rainfall is generally more than enough. However, by mid-May the weather is warming and the rainfall diminishing (May is the second driest month on average). It is during late May that furrow watering may be necessary to keep the lettuce growing well and keep it from becoming bitter.

I fertilize the beds with a 10-10-10 fertilizer prior to planting each section, and this is generally enough to make the crop. Iceberg-type lettuce requires more time, usually 2½ to 3 months, and a second application of fertilizer midway in the growth period.

Proper harvesting of lettuce is almost as important as proper growing. Lettuce is best taken in the morning when the leaves are turgid and before the sun hits the plants. Post-harvest handling is also important. The ice water bath recommended for broccoli is equally important for lettuce. After the bath, place one or two heads in a plastic bag to keep the leaves fresh and turgid when storing in the refrigerator.

PROBLEMS

Lettuce in the garden is seldom bothered by any insects or diseases. If rabbits are a problem, use bunches of human hair placed about the garden to repel them. To prevent any root problems, well-drained soil must be used and rotation is recommended.

❦ MELON
❦ Cucumis and Citrullus

HISTORY

Melons have always been a popular crop in the Southern garden. The muskmelon, which we now call cantaloupe, dates back to the earliest gardens, while the watermelon has been a part of Southern lore for years. Though neither is hard to grow, they do take space because of their long, widely-spreading vines.

There are many types of melons grown throughout the world, most unknown or rarely grown here. The traveler can become confused abroad because the cantaloupe of Europe and North Africa is different from the plant we know by that name. In the United States, the netted melons are commonly referred to as cantaloupe while the smooth melons are either Honeydew or Casaba. The watermelon is a quite different plant belonging to the genus *Citrullus* rather than *Cucumis*.

FORMS AVAILABLE

I have been a lover of melons from childhood days when my father would take me to the Monticello, Florida area to inspect the watermelon seed crop. It was a real adventure for me to walk the fields, always watching out for rattlesnakes, and partake of the talk and fun of adults. Every variety was always compared to *Stone Mountain*, a variety my father had introduced into the trade. There was nothing sweeter than a *Stone Mountain*, taken fresh from the field in the early morning, cut open and the heart removed to be tasted by us "experts." Never again has a watermelon been as sweet, until I found the small round watermelons of Egypt which even my dulled and aged taste buds told me were superior to my childhood favorite.

Cantaloupes are a different matter. They are all right, I suppose, but the flesh is too concentrated and the taste too strong to be one of my favorite fruits.

Honeydew melons are a different story. The large, smooth, creamy-white melons have light green flesh which has a unique and delicious flavor. The texture is like a fine "live" sherbert. Unfortunately, the honeydew takes a very long time to set and mature. During that three and one-half months many things can happen in the Southern garden to the detriment of this wonderful plant. But if you make it through all the vicissitudes of the muggy Southern summers, the results are worth every moment of time you have expended.

In Egypt and Morocco I found melons unheard of in the United States. These had such a delightful taste and a much better texture than cantaloupe. Each country of the Middle East and North Africa seems to have its own distinctive melon, all far superior to the cantaloupes we grow here.

Three of these melons, however, I thoroughly recommend if you can find the seed. *Charentais* is a French melon with many different strains. We grew them in Egypt and the small melons were distinctively textured and the taste superb. *Ogen* melon is one available in the United States with a unique texture and taste. One seed catalog describes its taste as that of Anjou pears. The last is an Israeli melon called *Gallia*. I tried some seed from an American company and found them totally lacking in uniformity. However, the growth, fruit set, disease-resistance, drought-resistance, and size of the fruit were remarkable. Some of the melons had that delicate flavor of the ones we grew in Egypt, but others tasted suspiciously like cucumbers. The Dutch seedsmen have the best strains. If you ever get a chance to purchase their seeds, do so. Your whole outlook on growing cantaloupe-type melons will change. The flesh is like a honeydew and of the same color, but the taste is like a rare sherbert.

In the South the biggest cantaloupe and honeydew problem is time. They take a long time to produce, and yet they cannot be planted in cold, wet ground. This means that the first ripe fruit will come after hot and dry weather which is not conducive to the most flavorful fruit. Being a hot weather type, *Gallia* seems to do much better under our summer conditions.

Watermelons are a different matter. They belong here in the South! Gardeners can grow them with few concerns except the necessary space.

CANTALOUPE AND HONEYDEW VARIETIES
Seed ½ Ounce per 50 Feet of Row, 1,000 Seed per Ounce

VARIETY	DAYS TO MATURITY	SPECIAL FEATURES
BUSH STAR HYBRID	88	Resistant to PM, very compact growth
SAMSON HYBRID	85	Early, resistant
EDISTO	95	Large fruit, strong grower, resistant to PM
EARLISWEET HYBRID	70	Very early, wilt-resistant
GALLIA	90	Unusual flavor, drought-resistant, heat-resistant
HONEYDEW	110	Long season

Note: PM = Powdery Mildew

WATERMELON VARIETIES
Seed ½ Ounce per 50 Feet of Row, 650 Seeds per Ounce

VARIETY	RELATIVE SIZE	DAYS	SPECIAL FEATURES
CHARLESTON GRAY	Large	87	Fusarium wilt-resistant
GARDEN BABY HYBRID	Small	78	Icebox type, compact growth
JUBILEE	Large	95	Wilt-resistant, striped fruit
SUGAR BABY	Small	75	Icebox type

PLANTING AND GROWING

All the melons are grown in the same basic way. They need loamy, well-drained soil that is not too rich or too high in nitrogen.

Plant melons as early as possible after the danger of frost has passed. Home gardeners do best by starting the seed in late March inside in peat pots or in cell packs. Allow the plants to develop in the cells or pots to the point when true leaves appear and a solid root mass has been formed, and then plant directly in the garden as soon as the frost danger has passed. Melons will grow in cooler temperatures than the seeds will germinate, and so several weeks may be gained by this procedure.

I plant melons on beds 2 feet wide with 5 feet between the edges. Plant the small plants in two rows with the plants staggered between the rows, giving a triangle pattern on the bed. The plants should be 2 feet apart in the row. Plant seeds the same way except plant three to five seed in a group with the groups 3 feet apart, again staggering the plantings between the two rows in the bed. When the seeds have germinated, thin to two plants per group.

Seeding must be done after the ground begins to warm or the seeds may fail to germinate. Watermelons are much more susceptible to poor germination in cold wet soil than the cantaloupes and honeydews.

Melons may be grown in hills that are 3 feet apart in the row. There should be 5 feet between rows. I have grown melons in hills and in beds and much prefer the bed method.

Use a 10-10-10 as a pre-plant fertilizer, and when the vines begin to run, use it again as a side-dressing. If any other fertilizer is needed, switch to a 6-12-12 or a 5-10-15 after blooms appear.

Cantaloupes are ripe when the vine "slips" cleanly from the melon. When melons are ripe there will be a definite odor and the heavily netted fruit will begin to take on a golden glow. Try pulling the vine out of the socket at the end of the fruit. If it comes cleanly or "slips," it is time to harvest. If it is hard to pull free, leave it for a few more days. Honeydew melons do not slip in the same way. They are harvested when the blossom end begins to feel as if it were "giving." If melons are to be stored in the refrigerator before eating, they should be given a cold water bath (see broccoli) to take the field heat out of the center. Store in the vegetable section of the refrigerator.

Every grower will give you a different way to tell when a watermelon is ripe. Thumping is fine if you know what to compare the thump noise with. Some say the tendril or pigtail which is closest to the melon will die when the melon is ripe; others say that the blotch on the underside will turn yellow when the melon is ripe. I harvest when the end begins to soften slightly, and there is a definite "give" when the end is pressed. The best way is to go into the garden in the early morning, thump a melon or two (for the fun of it), check the tendril to see if it is dead, press the end to see if it "gives," roll it over to see if the underside blotch is yellow, and pray a lot. You will soon know, because if it isn't ripe when the knife blade lays it open and everybody is eagerly waiting, your reputation as a gardener will drop to the bottom. Better luck next time!

Edisto Cantaloupe

Typical U.S. cantaloupe
with netting

Jubilee Watermelon

PROBLEMS

All melons are susceptible to a number of diseases, particularly powdery and downy mildew and wilt. Choose varieties which are resistant to as many of these diseases as possible and rotate plantings so that melons are not grown in the same spot more often than every three years. Melons are an ideal crop to follow fall broccoli or tomatoes. For further information on the control of melon diseases consult with your County Extension Service for their latest recommendations.

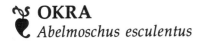

OKRA
Abelmoschus esculentus

HISTORY

I must admit that I do not like okra. That's a pity because okra has been identified as a Southern food since early colonial days, and it is easy to grow in the Southern garden. In New Orleans, gumbo with okra in it is a favorite dish. To me, it is worthless as a food and conjures up too many memories of hot August days in the fields of okra being grown for seed. One of my early jobs was cutting the dried pods for seed which my father's company sold. Every time I grow okra I remember those miserable days when the spines pierced my heavy khaki shirt and literally "ate me up."

I have never really been interested enough in the plant to find out its history until, when I arrived in Egypt and saw that okra was a standard dish, my curiosity overcame my prejudice. Bamiyah, as it is called, seems to have come from Khartoum in the Sudan and beyond, along the White Nile.

FORMS AVAILABLE

The Egyptians are adept at okra culture; the principal variety they grow is the very common Southern United States variety *Clemson Spineless*. Suddenly, okra has begun to appeal to many Americans other than just Southerners. There is now a flurry of work being done in the seed industry to hybridize okra, adapting it to wider use in gardens all over America. There are many new hybrids which are more dwarf and even more productive.

OKRA VARIETIES
Seed 1 Ounce per 50 Feet of Row

VARIETY	DAYS TO MATURITY	SPECIAL FEATURES
CLEMSON SPINELESS	56	Very strong, spineless pods
ANNIE OAKLEY	50	Early, compact plant
BLONDIE	55	Short, bushy, good yield

PLANTING AND GROWING

Mainly though, since okra is a crop for high temperatures and a long growing season, okra is ideal for the South. It does well in dry periods and has a remarkable ability to grow and produce fruit under very strained circumstances.

Plant okra in warm soil; it does not germinate in cold or cold, wet soil. So you must plant it at the end of the first warm crop-planting time. It is generally good to plant in furrows made in well-prepared soil, but if you must plant earlier, while the ground is still wet, plant in beds.

Sometimes the seeds are slow in germinating, especially when the ground temperature is below the 70s. If you soak the seeds overnight in tepid water, you can help start the germination process and produce a much better percentage of germinating seeds.

Work the ground well prior to planting, and apply 10-10-10 fertilizer. Plant as the ground really gets warm, opening a 4 or 5-inch-deep furrow and applying the fertilizer in the bottom. Work the fertilizer into the bottom of the furrow, drawing soil into the furrow from the sides until the bottom is about 1 inch deep, which is the proper planting depth for the seed.

Sow seed at the rate of about one ounce per 50 feet of row. After the seed germinates, thin the seedlings to a 12 to 15-inch spacing.

Okra should be grown at a rapid rate in its early formation period. I usually side-dress with ammonium nitrate when the plants are about 2 feet tall and beginning to bush. Once the flowers appear, continue monthly applications of fertilizer with a 6-12-12 type.

Okra will produce as long as the plant is growing well and setting flowers. Usually harvest will continue until the nights get cold in October.

Okra is tenderest, and considered to be best, when cut while the pods are still quite small. The maximum length for fresh pod curings is about 3 inches long, but most people consider the fingerling 2-inch pod the finest.

Okra is used in a variety of ways, including boiled, stewed, as an ingredient in soups, and with tomatoes in the famous Louisiana gumbo. Pickled okra is also quite popular. Probably the most delicious way to eat okra is sliced, dipped in a batter of egg and milk and then cracker crumbs, and fried. But all of these are for you, not for me! I'll grow it, but don't ask me to eat it.

PROBLEMS

It would be easy for me to say that the biggest problem okra has is just being okra, for there are few insect or disease pests which bother it. Occasionally, mildew will attack during muggy dog days in August, but seldom is it serious enough to warrant spraying.

In the Philippines, corn stalk borers migrated to the okra after the corn was removed and riddled some stalks. This may be a problem if the late summer is particularly muggy, but Bacillus Thuringiensis will give good control.

Nematodes are a serious problem. Always rotate plantings around the garden and never follow tomatoes, peppers, or eggplants with okra.

A well grown field of okra

Clemson Spineless Okra, a worldwide favorite

Clemson Spineless Okra is very productiv
and bears fruit over a long season.

Beltsville Bunching Onions are grown
for the tender tops.

Delta Giant Shallots

The "Vidalia Onion"

❧ THE GARDEN ONION
Allium cepa and other *Alliums*

HISTORY

The common large-bulb onion and its many relatives have been a part of man's diet throughout much of recorded history. The Egyptians grew them widely during the earliest Pharonic times and there are records (according to Herodotus) of their common use at the time the great Pyramid at Giza was built.

Our common onion and many plants closely related to it seem to have come from western Asia (*Hortus Third*) and were certainly known in Persia, Palestine, and Egypt from the earliest times.

In the South, a range of onion-type plants have been widely grown from colonial days. Our climate is well-suited to onion production, and it is a crop which readily overwinters in most of our area.

FORMS AVAILABLE

We grow not only the round-leaf onions like the common onion, shallot, multiplier onion, chive, and Japanese bunching onion, but also the flat-leaf types like garlic and leek. The planting and growing for all these onion and onion-related plants is similar and will be described together. The terminology for onions may be somewhat confusing since many of the old terms like "nest onion" and "tree onion" are still in use.

The **common onion** or **field onion** is grown from seeds or from small bunches of plants which have been started in seed beds and hardened off for transplanting. The field onion is sometimes grown from sets or small bulbs which are about 1/2 inch in diameter. These result from seedlings which are grown in beds and which are forced into dormancy artificially, usually by withholding water. The small bulbs may be held for a time and then planted in the garden, at which time their growth, which was arrested artificially, will begin again until they develop into the desired bulb-producing plant. The sets also are widely used to grow fresh, green onions which are called spring onions. These are grown for the tender, succulent tops which are chopped for salads.

The **shallot** is a type of onion which produces a unique "nest" of elongated bulbs with a distinct taste and flavorful leaves which may also be chopped for salads. The shallot is a specific type of onion (*Allium cepa*, Aggregatum group) with a distinctive taste quite different from the common onion, though, upon occasion, I have seen common nest onions and bunching onions sold as shallots. This belies the truth because true shallots are quite different, not only in taste but in looks.

The **multiplier** or Southern **nest onion** has been grown for generations here, usually being handed down from gardener to gardener. They are grown primarily for the green leaves which are present during the winter when their fresh taste is certainly welcome.

There are some onions which are called **tree onions**. These have a strong tendency to make small bulbs at the top of a stalk. They may be used for garnishing as well as propagation.

The **Vidalia Onion** which has become so famous in the market is not a different type of onion. It is one of the Spanish sweet onions which, when grown in the area near Vidalia, Georgia, produces a remarkably sweet, juicy onion of rare distinction. The variety commonly used is a *Granex* Hybrid. In most of the South, however, the distinctive flavor and mildness cannot be achieved since the climate of Vidalia is what makes the onion so good.

Large bulbous onions are divided into *SD* (short day) and *LD* (long day) types. When choosing varieties to plant in the South, the *SD* varieties are preferable since southern plantings are in the fall, winter and spring when the days are short. When checking seed catalogs or seed packets in stores, be sure and choose the correct day-length types.

ONION VARIETIES
Seed Count—9,000 per Ounce
200 Sets Will Plant 50 Ft. of Row

VARIETY	DAYS	TYPE	SPECIAL FEATURES
GRANEX HYBRID	80	SD	"Sweet" onion, light yellow, good taste
CRYSTAL WAX	95	SD	Mild white
BELTSVILLE BUNCHING	65	GO	Excellent spring onion for tops
DELTA GIANT SHALLOTS	—	—	Best for the South
ELEPHANT GARLIC	—	—	Largest garlic, very mild
EGYPTIAN TREE ONION	120	—	Crisp, bulbs in top

SD—Short Day or winter onion
LD—Long Day or summer onion
GO—Bunching type for green or spring onions

PLANTING AND GROWING

In the South, large bulb onions are grown during cool weather. Ideally, they should be planted in the fall, grown over the winter and spring, and harvested in the early summer. You can achieve fair success by planting them at the end of winter, usually mid-February, and harvesting them in June.

Green onions can be grown at almost any time except when it is hot. I like to plant onion sets in September and October to have green onions all winter, and to plant again in late February for additional supplies until the weather is hot.

You can plant shallots very soon after they are harvested and when they become available at garden supply stores. Since shallots do not store as well as the common onion set, they should be planted much sooner after harvest.

Onions need rich, loamy soil to produce big bulbs. When they are planted in furrows in heavy clay, the bulbs seldom attain a desirable size but remain elongated and skinny.

For best results, plant onions on a bed which is between 24 and 30 inches across, depending on whether you will be planting one or two rows on the bed. Rows on the bed should be 1 foot apart.

Apply a pre-plant fertilizer, using a 5-10-15 formula. Broadcast the fertilizer over the bed and work it in with a hand cultivator or a rake. Open a furrow just deep enough to accommodate the sets or plants. Plants to be grown into large onions should be spaced 4 inches apart. Sets to be grown for green onions should be planted 2 inches apart. If two rows are being made on the bed, triangulate the plants to give ample room for large bulbs to develop.

I use a 10-10-10 formula fertilizer for side-dressing when the plants are beginning to grow rapidly and the tops of the bulbs begin to show.

The secret of producing large onion bulbs is to keep them cleanly cultivated and the bed loose. As the bulb begins to develop, cultivate carefully between the rows on the bed and draw soil away, leaving the top of the bulb exposed. By harvest time only one-half the bulb may remain in the ground. This will also make a bigger bulb.

The flower stalk will appear long before the harvest. Pinch this away so that all the effort of the plant will be directed toward the production of the bulb.

Onions are ready for harvest any time the bulbs are large. Leave them in the ground as long as possible to produce the maximum size. Once the leaves begin to break and fall over, the plant is finishing its cycle and is ready for harvest.

Dig onions when the weather is dry. After removing them from the ground, spread them on newspapers and leave them in the garden until they are thoroughly dry and the skin is like paper. If this is not possible because of rain, spread them in a warm carport or garage. Leave the tops on the bulbs during this curing process. When the leaves and bulbs are dry or cured, cut off the tops about 1 inch above the bulb. Do not cut too close to the bulb, but leave enough of the dry top to act as a seal against rot which can start in the bulb. Handling onions before the skin dries will also cause bruising which invites rot. Do not wash onions to remove the dirt. Shake off as much as possible when digging and remove the balance after the skin has dried.

Store onions in mesh bags to allow air circulation around the bulbs. I like to hang the bags of bulbs in a cool, dry place like a basement or garage. Be sure not to let them freeze.

Grow, harvest, and cure other bulbous members of the onion family in the same way. You may grow garlic, shallots, nest onions, and tree onions with excellent success in the South. I even grow green or spring onions in the same way, merely planting the sets much closer together since I am going to eat the top and not the bulb. Grow leeks the same way on a bed with the plants spaced 3 to 4 inches apart.

Some gardeners like to plant onions from seeds. Because of serious disease problems, especially with germinating seedlings, you should do this in a cold frame or seed tray using sterile soil. It will take eight to ten weeks to produce plants for setting in the garden.

PROBLEMS

If other disease or insect problems occur, check with your County Extension Service for the latest means of control.

❦ PARSLEY
Petroselinum crispum

Parsley is said to have any number of excellent properties, but is used primarily to garnish food or to chop and add to soups. The most commonly-grown type is the moss-curled parsley which has very crinkled leaves.

Parsley is generally grown along with herbs since a few plants will be a gracious plenty for one family. It is actually a vegetable and not a herb, so I am treating it here.

Parsley is a perennial and will remain, most years, in the garden over the winter. However, because the most succulent and usable parsley leaves come from fresh new plants, most gardeners start new parsley each year.

Parsley is easy to grow but somewhat difficult to start from seeds since they may be slow germinating. You can overcome this difficulty by soaking the seeds overnight in warm water, then starting them in seed trays in the same way and at the same time you start cabbage. I then put my parsley in pots and hold the young plants in the greenhouse until early April, though a number of friends have had success planting them in the garden at the same time as beets and carrots.

You may grow parsley in flower beds also, but never plant it in an area where a systemic insecticide is to be used on nearby flowers or shrubs.

Regular fertilizing helps keep the foliage succulent and more desirable for the table.

Harvest a few leaves at a time whenever you need them, leaving the plant to continue growth and foliage production.

❦ PARSNIP
Pastinaca sativa

I have never grown parsnips and probably never will. In fact I have no desire to eat a parsnip, and as far as I know, I never have had. Yet Burpee lists them, so somebody must be growing parsnips somewhere.

Since the plant takes 105 days to mature, it is definitely not a plant for the spring garden. *Hortus* says the roots will not be good unless they develop in cool conditions. Thus, for you parsnip enthusiasts, parsnips should be a fall crop.

I suppose they should be grown in loose, fertile soil or on beds since they are a root crop and that is the way root crops are grown in the South.

That is all I am going to say about parsnips before I get into trouble.

PEAS

There are two kinds of "peas" grown in the South: the English pea or garden pea, *Pisum sativum*, and the cowpea, *Vigna unguiculata*, which is really a bean and not a true pea. Each has its own place in the garden cycle since the English pea is a hardy, cool-weather plant and the cowpea a tender, hot-weather crop. Both are leguminous and produce nitrogen for succeeding crops. Cowpeas are also useful as a green manure legume and are often grown as a summer cover crop, being turned into the soil before they become woody, and before the peas are mature.

ENGLISH or GARDEN PEA
Pisum sativum

HISTORY
The English pea has long been a garden favorite, first in Europe and then in the United States. They probably came from India or thereabouts and have been found in the tombs of the ancient Egyptians. Evelyn (1623) describes in great detail their cultivation in England, and so does Abercrombie (1823). White (1868) lists many varieties and describes how to grow them in the southern United States. In 1909 my grandfather listed eleven varieties, some of which are still grown today.

FORMS AVAILABLE
The South, however, has not usually been considered English pea country. The winters are traditionally too cold and the summers too hot for good development of the delightfully sweet wrinkled peas so prized farther north and in Europe. The best we have had in the South are smooth-seeded hardy varieties like *Alaska* which can be started in the dead of winter and allowed to mature before the weather is too hot.

The sweeter wrinkled peas are much less hardy and cannot be planted until the weather moderates. This causes them to mature after the weather begins to get too hot for the development of the sweetest peas. Only the quickest-maturing types should be planted. It is best to finish harvest by mid-June at the latest.

The edible podded peas, however, are different. This Oriental favorite has been widely grown in the South for many years; in fact, my grandfather listed two varieties in 1909. If you plant this type in January, by spring it is producing heavy crops of edible pods which are tender enough to be eaten raw in salads or cooked like beans.

Several years ago a whole new type of English pea was introduced. These are called snap peas. They are quite hardy and can be planted very early. The pods may be harvested while they are immature and eaten raw; allowed to mature a bit more, snapped like beans, and cooked; or allowed to mature fully and shelled like regular English peas. They are ideal for us since we can use them in several stages up until hot weather makes the peas tough and starchy.

The days to maturity will vary according to the temperatures during the winter and spring growing season. These numbers are strictly an average and should be used only as a guide.

ENGLISH PEA VARIETIES
Sow ½ lb. per 50 Feet of Row

VARIETY	CLASS*	DAYS	TYPE	SPECIAL FEATURES
ALASKA	S	55	Vine	Tends to be starchy, hardy
LITTLE MARVEL	W	63	Dwarf vine	Very early, wrinkled pea
PATRIOT	W	65	Vine	Early, wrinkled
WANDO	W	69	Vine	Heat-resistant
DWARF GRAY SUGAR	EP	65	Vine	Old favorite
SUGAR SNAP	SP	—	Vine	Multi-use

*Class
S = Smooth seeded, very hardy
W = Wrinkled seed, plant in spring
EP = Edible pod, very hardy
SP = Snap pea, winter and spring planting

PLANTING AND GROWING

English peas are grown when the weather is cool. They require rich, well-drained, fertile soil and a sunny, warm location when growing in the winter. Tight sticky soil causes peas to develop poorly and get a serious root-rot disease.

Plant English peas as quickly as possible in January. Work the soil deeply, to at least 10 inches, and open a furrow 8 inches deep. It is often said that to grow good peas you need to have a cow, for the bottom of the furrow should be lined with well-rotted or dehydrated cow manure. Cover the manure with 2 inches of soil and plant peas 2 inches apart. Draw an inch of loose soil into the furrow to cover the peas. As the peas begin to grow, gradually draw loose soil into the furrow against the stems until the furrow has been filled. Then side-dress with 6-12-12 fertilizer to keep plants growing rapidly whenever the weather is moderate.

There are two general types of peas: vine types and bush types. When growing vine types, plant a double row of peas side by side and place the support system between. When growing bush types, use a single row with rows at the standard 3-foot spacing.

The edible-podded peas can also be planted in the winter but may be planted in the spring since they are harvested at a less than mature stage.

The secret of having either type perform well is to grow them in cool weather and, once the weather moderates, to keep them well-fertilized and growing rapidly. When hot weather arrives, the pods become tough and the peas starchy. I prefer to switch from a 6-12-12 to a 10-10-10 fertilizer in late March.

PROBLEMS

English peas have few problems when grown at the correct time of year. You can avoid root-rot by planting in well-drained soil and rotating the garden so that there are three years between plantings in the same spot. Though in some seasons the pea aphid may appear, it is easy to control with Malathion.

Climbing English Peas with supports

Alaska English Peas are very hardy.

Cowpeas make an excellent hot weather cover crop.

Peanuts

Triple Moss Curled Parsley

❧ COWPEA
Vigna unguiculata

HISTORY

The cowpea of the South has been known by many different names over the years. I grew up calling it field pea and many still know it merely as black-eyed pea. It is actually a bean, very closely kin to the old-fashioned yard-long bean. There are over 200 varieties of this bean which have been identified.

Its origins are the Far East, probably China and India, though it has been known in Africa and the Middle East for centuries. Fortunately for us it has been a part of our Southern agriculture since the early days. White mentions it as strictly a Southern vegetable.

Cowpeas have wonderful names which are a recitation of things dear to our forebears. In early lists, and still surviving somewhat today, names like "The Quick Pea," "Whippoorwill," "Large Black Eye," "Wonderful," "Unknown," "Red Rippers," "Clays," "Iron," "Lady Peas," "Mississippi Silver," "Big Boy," "Blue Goose," "Calico," "Purple Hull," "Knucklehull," "Purple Hull Pinkeye," and "Worthmore" are nostalgic to those of us who grew up here.

Cowpeas mean a lot to the South because they are a truly multipurpose plant. In the late 19th and the early 20th centuries, the South was primarily rural and poor. The soil was worn out from continuous cotton cropping, and the people had little except what they raised themselves. The cowpea did two things for them. First, they were a marvelous cover and soil enrichment crop, and second, they were good food, both for stock and for humans. Cowpeas helped to bring Southern soil along the road back from near-depletion, while at the same time providing food for the table and for the livestock.

There is no less a need for this plant today than 100 years ago. Though we have attained a measure of human affluence, our soils are still near depletion, not this time from continuous cotton farming but now from the blade of the bulldozer. Top soil is ripped away to make new subdivisions, and once again we need "Whippoorwill" and "Iron Peas" to help us bring it back to life.

FORMS AVAILABLE

There are so many varieties of cowpeas being grown that it is impossible to say which is the best to grow. Each rural section has its favorite. Today, we generally grow whichever we can get at our local seed outlet.

My favorite is still the *Lady Pea*, which has every good attribute. But I must warn you that unless you have a pea sheller, the cook in your house isn't going to put up with the tedious shelling process of these tiny, tender peas. You shell, shell, shell and all you have is a handful of peas. But if the gardener will help do the shelling, the *Lady Pea* is a real treat for the table.

PLANTING AND GROWING

Cowpeas may be grown as a cover crop or as a row crop. I generally use it, in a measure, as both. After the spring crop has finished and when the ground has warmed, I till the parts of the garden from which the last of the winter and spring crops have been taken. I prepare a good seed bed with a rake and broadcast a

10-10-10 fertilizer lightly over the area, raking it in. I broadcast the seed at a rate of 3 to 5 lbs. per 1,000 square feet and cover lightly by raking again.

Then I turn under the succulent young plants as a green manure crop when preparing for August plantings of fall vegetables. Whenever possible, I leave a small block of cowpeas to mature so that I may harvest them.

Cowpeas may also be grown in rows in the garden. The procedure is the same as for furrow plantings of beans. This method of growing is for the peas rather than for a green manure crop since the stems become woody and tough the closer you get to the time of pea harvest. Cowpeas grown for the table are still worthwhile since they are a legume and add nitrate nitrogen to the soil.

✿ PEANUTS
Arachis hypogaea

I have grown peanuts, and it's fun! In fact, every gardener who has children should grow peanuts to let them watch this fascinating plant send the tube from the bloom down to the ground where the peanut is made.

The peanut is strictly a Southern plant in this country since it takes between 110 and 120 days to mature. So much of the Southern coastal plains are filled with peanut fields, one would think we could supply the world. However, the best tasting peanuts I have ever had were in the Meridien Hotel in Cairo, Egypt. The Egyptians grow a lot of peanuts, especially in the Aswan area, and they prepare them by burying them in the very hot sand. The ones at the Meridien were treated with salt in some way which partially glazed the skin. Before eating them, you rubbed the salty skin off and popped the kernel into your mouth. What a treat, though you certainly left a lot of skins in the ashtray.

The peanut is more properly classed as a commercial field crop and is grown in huge quantities throughout the South, and now through much of the tropical and semi-tropical world. I include it because of the unusual way of growing described above and because I think it is fun to grow, rather than because of any need to produce the peanuts which are so plentiful in our area.

Plant peanuts after the ground warms and there is no danger of frost. Think of planting peanuts at the same time you plant sweet potatoes. I grow peanuts on a bed which I keep loose through frequent cultivation. Use 10-10-10 as a pre-plant fertilizer worked into the bed. Open a 2-inch-deep furrow and plant the kernels (remove them from the shell before planting) about 4 inches apart. Thin the seedlings to 12-inch spacings. Side-dress two to three times during the growing season with a 6-12-12 or a 5-10-15 fertilizer.

After about three and one-half months, check the peanuts for size and dig them when they are mature. Dig the whole plant and let it air dry in a carport or basement. After the shells are firm and dry, remove the nuts from the roots. Now they are ready to boil or roast as needed. Next time I'm in Cairo, I will find out exactly how to prepare those delicious salted nuts and put it in the next edition of this book.

❦ PEPPER
❦ Capsicum sp.

HISTORY

One of Columbus' greatest achievements was the bringing of New World peppers to Spain in 1493. These plants were much different from the black and white condiment pepper of the Far East, which is in an entirely different class of plants, *Piper nigrum*. These New World peppers were enthusiastically received and soon became common plants of the continent, especially Spain. Both the sweet and the hot peppers of our gardens are in the genus *Capsicum* and I shall treat the two together.

Peppers are one of my favorite garden plants. For years I have collected many varieties of unusual pepper plants which I keep isolated to save pure seed each year. Some of these have most unusually-shaped pods and, over the years, have maintained wonderful Southern names like *Rooster Spur, Cowhorn, Little Boy, Christmas,* and one we introduced with the simple name of *Hastings' Hot.*

Many of these are just as suitable in the flower bed as in the vegetable garden. Their unusual pods make them delightful ornamental plants, yet the pods are suitable for hot sauces, hot jellies, and pickles.

The other group of peppers which is truly a vegetable garden plant is the Bell Pepper, called *Capsicum* in Europe. The large, blocky fruit can be used in any number of ways: fresh in salads, cooked and stuffed with meat, or chopped and cooked into all sorts of dishes.

Much work is being done to improve the Bell Pepper. The new highly-productive hybrids have larger fruit, more numerous fruit, and they come not only in the common green, but also in yellow and red. Some of the new hybrids are also resistant to more diseases than the open-pollinated varieties we have grown in the past.

FORMS AVAILABLE

PEPPER VARIETIES
4,500 Seed per Ounce

VARIETY	DAYS	TYPE	SPECIAL FEATURES
CALIFORNIA WONDER	75	Bell	Very dependable
YOLO WONDER	78	Bell	Very large
BELL BOY HYBRID	70	Bell	Early hybrid
KEYSTONE HYBRID	75	Bell	Very large
GOLDEN BELL HYBRID	68	Bell	Yellow fruit
SWEET BANANA	65	Long	Old favorite
PIMIENTO SELECT	95	Heart	Unique flavor
JALAPENO M	75	Hot	Very hot
CAYENNE, LARGE			
RED THICK	76	Hot	Long, hot
RED CHILI	85	Hot	Very hot

California Wonder Pepper

Bell Boy Pepper

Yolo Wonder Pepper

Christmas Ornamental Pepper

Flea beetles attack early peppers.

Jalapeno Pepper

There are many strains of open-pollinated varieties. I have grown each of those listed and have been extremely satisfied with the results.

There are a host of other types of peppers with special features like *Cubanelle, Hungarian Wax, Red Cherry,* and *Anaheim.* You may want to try some for the fun of it or for special recipes which you might have.

I have omitted ornamental peppers because of the huge number of varieties and types. Try some of them, and observe those in other gardens. They grow readily from seed. You can gather a single mature pod, dry it, and use it to start your own. Only a few of these varieties are commercially available.

PLANTING AND GROWING

Peppers are plants of warm temperatures and are quite susceptible to cold, especially when they are young. Gardeners should start seeds about six weeks before they are to be set in the garden, after the danger of frost. Young transplants should be stocky and strong but growing well. Do not harden them up in cold temperatures, however, because young plants with hard wood will take a long time to start growing again. I like to set my pepper plants when the weather is uniformly warm and not subject to sudden drops in temperature, especially at night. This later planting will also reduce the attacks of flea beetles, which can be a serious problem in cold weather.

Start seeds of peppers in a warm, sunny room six weeks ahead of planting. Set in the garden when the weather is uniformly warm.

Work the garden well and plant in open ground which has at least 6 hours of sun per day. I plant peppers the same way as tomatoes, on beds which are about 30 inches wide. Most varieties of peppers can be planted closer than tomatoes, or about 18 inches apart. You can increase the number per row by making two rows of peppers on the bed with the bed rows 12 to 15 inches apart. Triangulate the plants in the two rows to give ample space for them to develop.

Use a 10-10-10 as the pre-plant fertilizer and follow with side-dressings of 6-12-12 about every 6 weeks during the season. Peppers must be growing continuously and well to produce over a long season. In dry periods, water the beds thoroughly and keep up the fertilizer schedule during the whole season.

If you keep peppers cleanly harvested, new blossoms will continue to form and fruit will continue to be produced. Well-grown plants should produce until frost.

PROBLEMS

Peppers are subject to many of the soil-borne fungus diseases which attack tomatoes. Unlike tomatoes, however, there are no pepper varieties resistant to these diseases, so rotation is absolutely necessary. Never plant peppers in the same location where they or tomatoes have been grown within three years.

Some of the new pepper varieties have been developed with a resistance to Tobacco Mosaic Virus disease. Use these varieties whenever possible.

Peppers do have some insect problems, especially flea beetles in the early season. I have found good control of flea beetles with Diazinon.

❦ POTATO
Solanum tuberosum

HISTORY

The true potato or Irish potato is one of the most important food crops in the world today. It is widely grown from the sub-tropics to Scandinavia. Next to the cereal grains, it is probably the widest-produced food crop and by far the most heavily-produced vegetable in the world. Because it is the staple diet of millions, its fortunes or misfortunes have had an enormous effect on the peoples of the world. The famine in Ireland, which killed an estimated 750,000 people and forced so many immigrants to this country, was due entirely to the lack of potato production in 1845–1847 after the blight disease destroyed the potato crops.

The potato is native to the Andes in South America and its forebears still grow wild on the slopes of that great mountain range. It was also known in the earliest American colonies and introduced into Europe by the great explorers who marveled at its food properties. In England it was rather slow catching on. Evelyn does not mention it in 1675, but Abercrombie gives it much notice in 1823.

Despite their starchy nature, potatoes are not fattening, one 5-ounce tuber having only 90 calories. They also have considerable Vitamin C, significant protein, and many minerals. They are good for you. The French name, *pomme de terre*, meaning apple of the earth, says it well. This subterranean vegetable is truly a gift from the soil.

The edible portion is the thickened end of a rhyzome or underground stem called a tuber. The eyes which sometimes sprout on the shelf are latent buds which under proper conditions sprout in the way that the buds on the stem of a tree grow forth in the spring.

Potatoes are grown during both the spring and the fall here in the South. They are plants which produce tubers in cool temperatures and during short days. The soil should be rich, acid, drained, and loose enough for the tubers to form without difficulty or without becoming misshapen.

FORMS AVAILABLE

They are generally propagated from pieces of the tuber which have one or more of the buds or eyes present. Each piece of the tuber should weigh three or four ounces to give ample food for the new plant to start healthily. Recently, seedsmen have been advertising true potato seed which will produce plants and tubers as uniform as the vegetative pieces traditionally used. I have never planted these seeds, so I cannot report on their feasibility.

Any planting stock of Irish potatoes which you use should be certified free of diseases (certified seed potatoes) because the introduction of diseases through planting stock can be disastrous. It is not wise to use stock from your own garden because of the danger of reintroducing blight. It is not a good idea to use potatoes from the produce market, either, for most tubers which are sold in the market have been treated to prevent the eyes from sprouting in the home. This would keep the pieces from sprouting properly in the garden.

POTATO VARIETIES
3 to 4 lbs. of Seed Potatoes Plants 25 Feet of Row

KENNEBEC—White	WHITE COBBLER—White baking
RED PONTIAC—Red	SANGRE—Red

PLANTING AND GROWING

Spring-planted potatoes are one of our earliest crops. As soon as the hardest of freezes has passed, potatoes may be planted. The young sprouts are frost-hardy, and even if a late hard freeze burns them back, they will resprout. Planting early starts the crop quickly and allows them to mature before too-hot weather and while the days are shorter.

Grow Irish potatoes in loose soil; this means, in most cases, on a bed or ridge. You can plant them in a furrow, provided you ridge the soil against the young plants as they grow, giving the tubers the loose area in which they can form easily. Since most gardeners do not have plows to form the soil from the middle into a ridge, bed planting is the best answer. Use a tiller with a wing or hiller to form a bed at least 24 inches to 30 inches wide and 10 inches high. The distance between the beds should be enough for the tiller and hiller attachment to work easily. Use a 10-10-10 formula as the pre-plant fertilizer, worked into the bed prior to planting. Open a furrow about 4 inches deep in the middle of the bed. Place the pieces of the seed potatoes about 8 inches apart in the furrow and cover them.

Several sprouts will come from each piece and will grow quickly. Keep working the space between the beds with a tiller and hiller, continuing to raise the height of the bed until it is about 12 to 15 inches high. Remove the hiller and continue cultivating with the tiller alone. This keeps the soil on the bed loose, allowing the tubers to develop properly.

Potatoes are heavy "feeders" and need continued fertilizing with a 10-10-10 every four to six weeks to make a good crop.

Potatoes are ready to harvest whenever the tubers have reached a size you like. Most gardeners, however, wait until the vines begin to die before digging. After this the tubers will not increase in size. In the fall it is wise to let the first frosts kill the tops before digging. But do not let the ground freeze before removing the tubers. Any frost which reaches the tubers will cause decomposition. A good way to know that there are sizable potatoes under the ground is to watch for heavy cracks in the surface of the bed.

Remove the clumps of potatoes carefully and separate the tubers from the stems and tops. Shake off the excess soil but do not wash or rub it off before the skin toughens. Spread the freshly-dug potatoes on dry newspaper in a dark place for a week to toughen the skin. Then remove the rest of the soil and store the potatoes for later use in a dry, cool (40–50 degree) place.

PROBLEMS

There are many insects which attack potatoes, the most disastrous being the Colorado potato beetle. Flea beetles, leaf hoppers, and aphids may also present problems. Check with your County Extension Service for the latest recommendations for controlling these pests.

Potatoes are best grown on beds.

Chris Hastings with his first crop of radishes

Potatoes are grown from eyes on these sections.

Harvest radishes when small and crisp.

Cherry Belle Radish

The major diseases of potatoes are late blight, early blight, and scab. The planting of certified seed potatoes will greatly reduce the blight problem with the spring crop, since the blight generally attacks about the time the plants are ready for harvest. Protect the fall crop with regular sprayings of a fungicide since the blight disease will be prevalent at that time. Consult the recommendations of your County Extension Service for the best sprays for your area.

Scab is a serious problem if the pH of your garden soil is too high. The disease does not spread in low pH soil. Never lime soil in which potatoes are to be planted because this will increase the soil pH level and encourage scab.

The tubers of the potato should always remain covered with soil or they will turn green. This condition makes the potato taste bitter and can be somewhat dangerous as toxins develop in the green fruit. Keep soil pulled over the area where the tubers are growing to keep the fruit covered.

RADISH
Raphanus sativus

HISTORY

Radishes must be cultivated by humans, for they do not occur in the wild, and they seem to have been with us forever. The ancient Chinese, Egyptians and Greeks all grew the radish.

Now radishes are grown primarily as a salad food or garnish rather than an important staple of the diet. The crisp, clean flesh with a mildly pungent flavor is much prized for these purposes. Fortunately the radish is one of the easiest to grow of all garden plants.

FORMS AVAILABLE

RADISH VARIETIES
Sow 1 Ounce per 100 Feet of Row; 2,500 Seeds per Ounce

VARIETY	DAYS	COLOR	SPECIAL FEATURES
CHERRY BELLE	22	Red	Most popular
CHAMPION	28	Red	Good keeper
ICICLE	28	White	Summer radish, 5 inches long
APRIL CROSS HYBRID	60	White	18 inches long, remains tender

PLANTING AND GROWING

Though there are summer and winter varieties used by gardeners in other regions of the United States and abroad, here in the South radishes are almost exclusively the domain of spring and fall.

The only particular consideration in growing radishes during these seasons is a loose, friable soil, fertilizer to force quick growth, and a good variety. In three to five weeks the radishes are ready for harvest. No wonder they are the delight of first-time gardeners and children, for it seems as though the seed are barely in the ground before the radishes are on the table.

Since radishes are grown for their roots, I grow them on a bed just like turnips that are grown for roots and not just for salad greens. The bed does not have to be as wide as for turnips; 18 to 24 inches is ample. Since radishes mature so rapidly and are best when pulled at their prime rather than left in the ground for any length of time, don't sow too many at once. Instead, plant short rows a week apart. It is also possible to plant two rows on a 24-inch bed.

Another good way to plant radishes is to interplant them with longer maturing crops like broccoli or onions which are grown in double rows on a bed. Plant a single row of radishes down the middle of the bed between the two rows of the main crop.

You can plant radishes as soon as the hardest freezes have passed. They will germinate in cool soil and grow when frost, even light freezes, are occurring. Plant fall radishes in September for October and early November harvest. They will grow in a number of soil types but for best results plant in beds to allow quick, tender root development.

Apply a 6-12-12 fertilizer prior to planting. Open a very shallow furrow and seed rather thickly (seed are very inexpensive). Plant seed about 1/2 inch deep. After the seeds are up and growing, thin to a stand with seedlings about 3 inches apart.

I know some gardeners who plant radishes in blocks on the bed. They measure off three or four feet of the bed, apply the 6-12-12 fertilizer, and rake it into the soil. Then they broadcast the seed over the part of the bed set aside for radishes and lightly rake the seed into the soil.

Interplanting of radishes with taller-growing spring crops like broccoli is a real space-saving gardening practice. After the broccoli has been set on the bed, open a shallow row down the middle and plant the radishes as if they were planted alone. The fertilizer generally used for broccoli and other spring crops is 10-10-10 rather than the 6-12-12 I recommended for radishes. Do not be concerned; the fertilizer applied for the broccoli or other crops will be satisfactory to grow your radishes.

Harvest as soon as the radishes are an inch or inch and one-half in diameter. If the weather has warmed at harvest time, radishes will keep crisp longer in the refrigerator when they are given the cold bath treatment in the sink before refrigerating.

PROBLEMS

Radishes have few problems. However, it is wise to rotate the crop to prevent any root maggot damage. Never plant radishes in the same spot in the spring and fall of the same year. Aphids may also attack if you are late planting. Diazinon is a good aphid control.

❦ RHUBARB
❦ *Rheum Rhabarbarum*

Here is another plant I have never grown and must depend on others for information. Like parsnip information, this is for you and not for me, since even the pies of
my good friend Ruth Beasley, which were oohed and aahed over by many, were
something I could easily have done without. In case you have just arrived from the
North, I will pass on all I can garner about this "Yankee" vegetable.

My associate in the seed business, Loy Thomas, grew rhubarb for some years.
His advice was to grow it on beds in a cool part of the garden which had afternoon
shade. My friends the Beasleys, who made the pies, gave up their rhubarb after
several years because of its poor growth in the South.

Rhubarb needs constant growing conditions during the season and should be
fertilized and watered on a regular basis. Use a 6-12-12 fertilizer to keep it growing well and use furrow watering between the beds.

Plant rhubarb roots in the winter whenever they are available and when you
can prepare the beds. Set the roots on 30-inch beds three feet apart in the row.

If you are setting only a few plants, it is advisable to keep the bed well-
mulched to prevent weed problems and to conserve moisture.

That is all I know or want to know about rhubarb; for harvesting and cooking
information, you must check elsewhere.

❦ SOYBEAN
❦ *Glycine Max*

The soybean has become one of the world's most important economic crops. It is
primarily an agricultural crop with interest to the gardeners of this country only
recently, though it has long been a garden vegetable in the Orient.

Grow soybeans just as you would bush beans and for detailed culture, see that
section. The main considerations and deviations from standard bean production are
that soybeans take about three months to mature and cannot be planted in as cold
ground as snap beans. Plant soybeans about the time you plant okra.

Edible soybeans may be used like snap beans or edible-podded peas by harvesting in the immature green stage. The Orientals, however, allow the beans to
mature more fully and harvest them just before the pods start yellowing. The pods
are then boiled in salty water and shelled at the table as they are eaten. Also, you
can allow them to mature completely on the plant and store them dry. Later you can
prepare them like dry lima beans.

❦ SPINACH
❦ *Spinacia oleracea*

HISTORY

In the South, spinach has never been the green vegetable it has been in other parts
of the country. The turnip is our green, while spinach holds that distinction elsewhere. Popeye and the resulting admonition from mothers to "eat your spinach so

you will be strong like Popeye" ruined the flavor of this wonderful green for several generations of children.

Spinach is making a tremendous comeback on the table, though, with the introduction of raw spinach salads and the health food craze.

This vegetable has been around a long time, originally coming from Southeast Asia and showing up in England in the 1500s. Essentially, it has always been used as a boiled green until the recent raw salad craze. Now it is seen in salad bars as much as in the pot.

FORMS AVAILABLE

SPINACH VARIETIES
2,900 Seeds per Ounce; 1 Ounce per 100 Feet of Row

VARIETY	DAYS	LEAF SHAPE*	SPECIAL FEATURES
MELODY HYBRID	42	Semi-savoyed	Blue mold, virus-resistant
TYEE HYBRID	39	Savoyed	Blue mold-resistant
BLOOMSDALE LONGSTANDING	50	Savoyed	May overwinter

*Savoyed-Heavily crinkled

PLANTING AND GROWING

Spinach is a cool-weather vegetable which must be grown in the South in the spring or fall so that harvest occurs while the temperatures are low. Otherwise spinach will quickly produce a heavy stalk, tough leaves, and a seed head.

The spring crop has traditionally been the best one for us, since harvest would come before attacks of blue mold, a powdery mildew disease which quickly ruins the plant. The recent introduction of blue mold-resistant varieties has made the fall crop much more feasible and one well worth your time and effort.

Spinach can be grown on beds in the spring or in furrows if that is the way your garden is set up. The important thing is to plant as early as possible after the hardest freezes have passed. I plant spinach in early March on beds and grow it off rapidly, to be replaced with other early summer vegetables or New Zealand spinach, which can take the heat.

A 30-inch bed will accommodate two rows of spinach 15 inches apart. When sowing in well-prepared soil you may make the drills as close as 12 inches apart.

The soil should be thoroughly pulverized since the seed are small and must be planted only about one-half inch deep. A pre-plant application of 10-10-10 fertilizer will probably grow the crop, though one additional application may be needed to keep the plants succulent and growing rapidly.

After the soil is pulverized, the beds made, and the area fertilized, open a very shallow furrow so that the seed will be only one-half inch deep when the furrow is covered. Seed continuously (drill) in the furrow at the rate of one ounce per 100 feet of row.

Disoy edible soybeans

Melody Hybrid Spinach

Yellow Summer Crookneck Squash

Senator Zucchini Squash

Summer squash, the South's favorite

After germination, thin to a stand of healthy plants 4 to 5 inches apart.

To harvest spinach, cut off the whole plant at ground level and take it to the kitchen, washing it and preparing it for the salad or pot immediately. Spinach will keep in the crisper for many days, and freezes well. When the weather is warm, a cold water bath will increase the keeping time.

PROBLEMS

The two major problems of spinach are blue mold (powdery mildew) and virus. The timing of your crop and the planting of resistant varieties usually eliminates any need for chemical controls.

NEW ZEALAND SPINACH
Tetragonia tetragonioides

This fabulous and productive green I have grown often in place of spinach for late April and May plantings. It will grow well during hot weather, and you can remove the leaves from the plants as you need them, allowing the plant to remain and continue production. The leaves are somewhat more stiff than regular spinach and are not as satisfactory for raw spinach salads. However, when it is cooked the taste is identical.

Plant New Zealand spinach after you harvest regular spinach or in late April or early May. I plant mine in beds since this is the way my regular spinach is grown and the way my garden is arranged at this time. I have planted in shallow furrows in well-prepared soil with the rows far enough apart to cultivate. On the bed, I plant only a single row since the plants will spread more than regular spinach.

Sow the seed in drills, covering them about 1/2 inch. Thin the plants to an 8 to 12-inch spacing and grow them rapidly, continuing to fertilize and water when necessary.

SQUASH AND PUMPKIN
Cucurbita pepo and other species

HISTORY

Botanically, squashes and pumpkins fall into the same four species of *Cucurbita*. Examples of each are found in each of the groups, therefore the common names can be confusing when you try to place each type correctly.

When you live in one spot all your life what you call squash and what you call pumpkin is no problem. To the Southerner, squash means yellow summer squash. To most Northerners, squash means baking squash like butternut and acorn. You can realize my dilemma when I got to Egypt and found that those beautiful plants growing in the Nile Delta I thought were squash were a strangely-fruited plant which produced a hard fruit for drying. From these the seeds were extracted and roasted for a delightful snack.

In Europe, where yellow summer crookneck squash is virtually unknown, you find vegetable marrows (similar to baking squash) and courgette, which is our zucchini.

Hortus Third simplifies it best. Summer squash is harvested immature and generally boiled, while winter squash is harvested when mature and baked. I guess pumpkins are round, orange (or yellowish-tan), and from them Jack-O-Lanterns are made.

In the South, squash stands for yellow crookneck or straightneck; zucchini has been widely grown only recently. Acorn and butternut have also been used over the years but not in the quantity of yellow summer squash.

Nonetheless, the importance of squash of whatever kind is tremendous for the gardener. They are very productive, easy-to-grow vegetables which can be eaten in a number of ways besides baked and boiled. My wife makes a zucchini casserole which is sublime. Nowadays, zucchini and crookneck squash show up in raw salads and also as a vehicle for a tasty dip.

Since squash bears heavily, a few plants will yield enough (or more than enough) for a family. In fact, a great deal has been written about the dilemma of the gardener with too much zucchini. It can be a problem. I have found myself with mountains of zucchini as a result of my ambitious effort to try growing some new varieties.

FORMS AVAILABLE

In the South there are still a number of "squash" which have been handed down over many generations and which serve some strange and wonderful purposes. I have grown the "healing" squash, which has an enormous vine, growing all over the garden while producing large fruit, excellent for baking. These are harvested as needed and before the skin is dry. The end section may be cut, leaving the rest

SQUASH VARIETIES
Summer, 200 Seed per Ounce; Winter, 120 Seed per Ounce

VARIETY	DAYS	TYPE	SPECIAL FEATURES
YELLOW SUMMER CROOKNECK	53	Summer crookneck	Old favorite, still excellent
DIXIE HYBRID	41	Summer crookneck	Early crookneck, very prolific
AMBASSADOR HYBRID	51	Summer zucchini	Dark green, prolific
SENATOR HYBRID	41	Summer zucchini	Medium green, prolific
TABLE ACE HYBRID	70	Winter acorn	Semi-bush, stores well
WALTHAM HYBRID	90	Winter butternut	Dark orange, stores well

The immature squash can be seen below the female flower.

Yellow Crookneck Squash is most tender when young.

Ambassador Hybrid Zucchini Squash

Squash vine borer

Male blossom of squash. Note the anthers of pollen.

Big Max field pumpkin

PUMPKIN VARIETIES
100 to 300 Seed per Ounce

VARIETY	DAYS	SIZE	SPECIAL FEATURES
BIG MAX	120	100 lbs.	Jack-O-Lantern type
SMALL SUGAR	100	6 lbs.	Best eating
SPIRIT HYBRID	100	10 lbs.	Semi-bush type

to continue growing fresh on the vine for later use. Hence the name "healing" squash, for the end left on the vine seals and thus heals itself.

Many of these so-called squash types are actually edible gourds, while others like the cushaws are in the squash-pumpkin group of *cucurbits*.

PLANTING AND GROWING

All squash and pumpkins are tender plants which do not like cold soil or cold air. Even the lightest frost on your plants will ruin them. They should be planted after all danger of frost has passed and when the ground temperature is warm. The summer squash produce in a relatively short time while most winter squash take approximately three months to mature.

The seeds of squash are large and susceptible to poor germination in cold, wet soil. To overcome this, I plant squash as soon as frost has passed but on beds to have a warmer, dryer growing area. Early planting may also be successful if the seed are started inside in cell packs and transplanted into the garden after frost danger.

Squash and pumpkins may be started ahead of time in order to have plants to set in the garden as soon as the ground warms. Frankly, I have never found this to be the best, because these plants grow extraordinarily fast in a sunny window, and, if allowed to become too large before setting, they will be slower in growing off than if seed were planted. If you want to try this method, be sure to plant in cells so that the seeds germinate in the medium in which they will grow until they are set in the garden. Do not try to pot tray-grown seedlings because the shock of transplanting will destroy any time edge you've gained.

If you are not making beds for other crops and are planting in furrows only, you can make hills to provide the same type of condition which occurs in bed planting. In fact, the use of hills with squash and melons was the standard method of planting in the old South. Many still follow the practice now.

Prepare the soil well and use a 10-10-10 as a pre-plant fertilizer. Work this into the bed or into the furrow before making the hills.

Squash grow large. The bush types may be planted in groups of three to five seeds about 3 feet apart or in hills at the same spacing. Since acorn and other baking squash tend to spread more, they should be spaced about 4 feet apart.

After germination, thin to the two best seedlings per group or hill. Watch the young seedlings carefully. If the cotyledons (seed leaves) look as though they are drying up before the true leaves are growing rapidly, inspect the plants in the early morning for the spotted or striped cucumber beetles which attack these baby plants with a vengeance. If you don't dust immediately with Sevin or Diazinon, you will have to replant.

Keep squash growing rapidly by fertilizing at least every six weeks. At this stage, however, I prefer a 6-12-12 fertilizer as a side-dressing.

Growing pumpkins follows the method of growing squash except that the spacing is much greater for these viney plants. The groups or hills for pumpkins should be 6 feet apart and the rows 6 feet apart. The fruit of pumpkins should be dusted frequently as they begin to enlarge to prevent the fruit worm from boring into the soft underside. In a small pumpkin patch, place a piece of plastic underneath each baby pumpkin to prevent the worms from coming from the soil underneath.

Summer squash of all varieties should be constantly picked to keep bloom and fruit coming. The size of the fruit to pick is your choice. "The smaller the more tender" is not the case now with the new hybrids. The old Italian black zucchini, for instance, would become very tough and the seed large if it was eight inches long. The new hybrids are just as tender and the seed just as small at eight or even ten inches as they are at five.

Leave winter or baking squash on the vine until the plants begin to die and the skin of the fruit is hard. Leave pumpkins forever, it seems, until the vine dies and the skin is hard also.

PROBLEMS

One of the confounding things about squash which drives the unknowing gardener crazy, as well as those of us in the advice-giving business, is the way the early blooms fall off without producing fruit. When this happens, the unscrupulous garden supply dealer may make a small fortune with all kinds of fruit-setting materials. By the time the gardener gets around to spraying, the results are amazing. As if by magic (or, it is thought, by chemical results), the young squash appear in droves. The same results could have been attained by spraying water on the blooms or, better yet, doing nothing, for squash has the peculiar habit of setting enormous numbers of male flowers for quite some time before the first female flowers are produced. This peculiarity is found in a number of the *cucurbits* including cantaloupes and cucumbers, so remember that patience is better than spraying.

The major problems of squash are the striped and spotted cucumber beetles, the squash vine or stem borer, and mildew. Fortunately, these problems seem to occur one after the other and not all at the same time or all the same year, necessarily. Once past the seedling stage, normal dusting with Sevin will keep the cucumber beetles under control. If you will dust the inside of the plant and the stem as it comes from the ground, you can control the vine borer.

The vine borer damage will not be noticed until one day when the leaves of those beautiful big plants begin to droop as if the plants were in a two-month drought. Once this happens, it is difficult to control the pest. However, I have carefully split the stem as it comes out of the ground, removed the ugly beast, and wrapped the slit portion with waterproof tape, saving the plant for continued production.

Frankly, I don't pay much attention to mildew because, by the time it hits in my garden in mid-August, I am sick to death of squash and just pull up the plants.

However, there are some gardens in my area where the air circulation is so poor that mildew strikes before the gardener gets sick and tired of eating and freezing squash. There are two basic types of mildew which attack squash: powdery mildew which is white, and downy mildew which is gray. Identify which one you have and check with your County Extension Service for the best control. The material is different for each of these.

⚘ SWEET POTATO
Ipomoea Batatas

HISTORY

When my boys were 3 and 5 years old, I took them to the garden to help me dig sweet potatoes. I shall forever remember the screams of glee as they dove into a clump of earth, retrieving the lumps of golden roots. Betsy said it was just like mining for gold, and their reaction showed that no nuggets of gold could have thrilled two young boys any more. For this and many other reasons, I like to grow sweet potatoes. They are one of the bounties of the Southern garden—easy to grow and highly productive.

I have lived most of my life with the firm belief that sweet potatoes should be red to golden in skin color with a deep orange flesh. *Georgia Red* was a sweet potato; what was grown in New Jersey was something else entirely. It took a trip to England to discover the white sweet potato which Englishmen of Caribbean extraction believe to be the only decent one. To my surprise, Rosa Weems, my authority on old Southern country plants, tells me that her father grew white sweet potatoes in central Georgia many years ago.

The sweet potato is probably of New World origin but is now grown in practically all tropical and sub-tropical countries as one of the most important food sources. It is a member of the morning glory family, and its rarely-seen bloom looks like the wild morning glory which plagues the garden. Being a perennial which is used as a long-standing annual, it is propagated from shoots called slips which arise from adventitious buds formed on the swollen root, rather than from seed (which seldom form). The edible part is this swollen root which is used by the plant as a large storage organ. It is physiologically different from the Irish potato, which is a tuber or swollen end of a rhyzome or underground stem. The sweet potato is part of the underground root system and has no eyes to sprout.

Sweet potatoes have been grown in the South since the early colonial days. White in *Gardening for The South* gives extensive instructions for its culture and lists several varieties, including *Hayte*, which is listed as a white. He also states that this vegetable came to England in 1597 and is the potato mentioned in Shakespeare, since the Irish potato was virtually unknown at the time. However, neither Evelyn nor Abercrombie mention it as an English garden plant, and even today, the English climate is not conducive to its culture.

FORMS AVAILABLE

SWEET POTATO VARIETIES
Set Plants 18 Inches Apart

BUSH PORTO RICO (bush type)	CENTENNIAL (vine type)
GEORGIA RED (vine type)	VARDAMAN (bush type)

PLANTING AND GROWING

The sweet potato requires at least four months to produce a satisfactory crop. Plantings may be made through June in the South. Traditionally, harvest is in October when the frost burns the tops, though care should be taken not to leave them in the ground when there is a chance of freezing. The potatoes are very susceptible to cold and should be removed and cured at warm temperatures. Storage should be at warmer temperatures than Irish potatoes or above 55 degrees F.

Plant sweet potato slips after the ground is warm, usually in early to mid-May. The soil should be well-prepared and well-drained. Do not add animal manures to the soil in large quantities, for they carry problems which reduce yields. Also, never plant sweet potatoes in garden areas where tomatoes, peppers, melons, or other plants highly susceptible to nematodes have been grown, since these pests attack sweet potatoes with a vengeance.

Plow or till the garden area thoroughly and form a bed about 30 inches wide. Make the beds at least 3 feet apart or far enough apart for constant cultivation. Work 10-10-10 fertilizer into the bed prior to setting out the slips. Sweet potato slips look pretty pitiful and may have some trouble becoming established unless you give them a little extra care. I learned a very helpful practice from a great planter, Wilbert Grissom, who taught me to dig a shallow hole at the end of the row in loose soil. Fill this with water, and when the hole has become a wet, muddy mess, put the roots of the slips in it. Coating the roots like this protects them and helps the plants to start more quickly, giving a better "live." Open a small hole in the row, deep enough to accommodate the roots of the slip. Space the holes 18 to 24 inches apart. Drop the slip in the hole and cover the roots. If the soil is dry, water each hole well to settle the soil around the roots and protect them from drying as the new hair roots begin to grow.

Keep sweet potatoes growing rapidly with fertilizer (5-10-15 or 6-12-12) and free from weed and grass competition. Cultivate them frequently to keep the bed loose, allowing the potatoes to form well. In periods of drought, keep them growing by irrigating between the rows and allowing the water to move into the bed from the edges.

The soil next to the plant will begin to crack when the potatoes are forming. Don't harvest too early or too late. Sweet potatoes take from 120 to 150 days to make good-sized bakers, and the longer you can leave them, the better. I dig my sweet potatoes after the first October frost has nipped the leaves.

Dig them carefully! Bruising or cutting the potatoes invites rot and prevents good storing. I use a spading fork and dig into the bed from the side, underneath

Chris and Don, the author's sons, digging for gold—sweet potatoes.

Monte Carlo

Small Fry

Packing truly mature tomatoes at the author's Egyptian desert project.

The sucker below the first bloom cluster should be left.

the plants. Lift the clumps out and lay them aside until they have all been dug. Carefully take the clumps to a very warm, dry spot inside a basement or garage, and then separate them and spread them out to cure. Curing is best done at about 80 degrees and for 12 to 15 days. This toughens the skin and prevents rot. After curing, cook or freeze any potatoes with cuts or bruised areas which may already be turning dark, since they will not store well.

Well-cured sweet potatoes can be stored for five or six months without any difficulty. Store in a place where the temperature never goes below 55 degrees F.

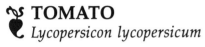 TOMATO
Lycopersicon lycopersicum

HISTORY

The tomato is by far the most popular vegetable grown in American gardens. It seems redundant to describe it in detail because almost everyone who has even a tiny plot of soil has at least one tomato plant and detailed ideas about its culture. A fellow Atlantan has even written a book on this subject alone, and in almost every garden series there is a book on this plant's culture. New ideas and techniques are practiced first on tomatoes, then on other plants.

My approach to tomato-growing is like my approach to most garden plants. I don't believe in getting carried away and changing a successful practice or variety just for the sake of accepting a suggestion. I enjoy gardening too much to be greatly influenced by anything I haven't tried personally. What I write is the result of many years of experience and trial. Take it for what it is: the experience of yet another gardener.

The tomato is a relatively recent introduction into American gardens as a whole. Though it was mentioned by Thomas Jefferson as being grown in colonial days, it was still thought in Massachusetts to be poisonous at a time when it was widely grown in England (Abercrombie's *Practical Gardener*, London, 1823). The plant is of South American origin, and was widely grown as far north as Mexico by the Mayan Indians (Sturtevant's *Notes on Edible Plants*).

By the beginning of the 20th century, the tomato was an extremely popular horticultural plant, widely grown as a commercial crop as well as in the home garden. My grandfather listed 19 varieties in his catalog of 1909, a very respectable number even by today's standards.

The popularity of the tomato comes from several factors. First, it is an easy plant to grow; second, it produces well; third, one or two plants can produce enough to feed two people over many months; and fourth, the quality of the home-grown fruit far exceeds that generally found in the market.

The problem with commercially-grown tomatoes is that they are fragile when they are at their peak in taste. So the commercial growers pick them green (they call it mature, but they are still green) and ripen them by treating them with ethylene gas to turn them red. When the unsuspecting consumer eats the tomato, he or she believes they are eating a ripe tomato because it looks ripe when actually it is still far from ripe.

Being far more discerning than Americans, Europeans and Middle Easterners will not tolerate gas-ripening. On our farm in Egypt we grew as many as 500 acres of tomatoes at a time. The packs for Europe had to be a full pink color (with absolutely no gassing). We wrapped each tomato in tissue to protect its fragility. Our percentage of first-quality fruit for packout was far below that of our American counterparts because we couldn't pass green tomatoes off on the European consumer. Americans, tired of the tasteless market tomatoes, turn to the garden for the delicious red ripe fruits which add so much to any meal.

FORMS AVAILABLE

One quick glance at a seed catalog or a trip to the nursery or plant shop will convince you that varieties and types can confuse even the best gardener. There are several distinctions among tomatoes that the gardener should know about before choosing a variety.

Tomatoes are classified in two general and two specific ways. Generally speaking, there are the large-fruited varieties like *Better Boy, Monte Carlo,* and *Celebrity,* and the small-fruited varieties like the cherry, plum, and pear varieties. The specific classification, which encompasses both the large-fruited and small-fruited groups, is whether a variety is indeterminate or determinate.

Indeterminate tomatoes are varieties which continue to grow predominantly from the main stem. They are sometimes referred to as vine tomatoes because they form a vine which has to be staked. The determinate tomatoes grow almost equally from the lateral stems and the main stems. They are referred to as self-topping or bush varieties. In the lexicon of the commercial growers, there are also various grades of determinate varieties, like strongly determinate (very bushy) and semi-determinate (more upright and needing support).

It is important for the gardener to know which class his varieties are. Determinate varieties generally do not produce over as long a period of time as the indeterminate varieties do. In our Egyptian fields we planned for a 4 to 6-week harvest from the determinate varieties and an 8 to 12-week harvest from the indeterminate varieties.

Determinate varieties also need less support. They may be caged or tied to a single stake with ease, whereas the indeterminate varieties need stakes and string or some very tall support.

Tomato varieties differ tremendously in their amount of fruiting and in their disease-resistance. Because of their popularity, there has been much genetic work done on the improvement of tomatoes. Certain keys or symbols have been added to a name to advise the grower about the specific properties of that variety.

The word hybrid following a variety name means that specific genetic work has been done to make improvements of one type or another. In general, hybrid varieties are more productive and have specific disease-resistant factors bred in which help the gardener.

The three most troublesome problems of tomatoes are found in the soil. These are verticillium wilt, fusarium wilt, and nematodes. Varieties with the letters VFN following the name are resistant to these three terrible problems, a distinct advantage to the home gardener who may have neither the room nor the inclination to

TOMATO VARIETIES
9,000 Seeds per Ounce

VARIETY	DAYS	TYPE	DISEASE RESISTANCE	SPECIAL FEATURES
CATEGORY I				
*BEEFMASTER (H)	80	Indet.	VFN, ASC, St.	Very large
*BETTER BOY (H)	75	Indet.	VFN, ASC, St.	Heavy producer
*BIG SET (H)	70	Det.	VFN, ASC, St.	Bush-type
CELEBRITY (H)	70	Det.	VFN, ASC, St., TMV	Bush-type, large fruit
CONTESSA (H)	72	Det.	F, N, ASC, St., TMV	Large fruit
DUKE (H)	74	Det.	V, F., ASC, St.	Large fruit
FLORAMERICA (H)	70	Det.	V, F, ASC, St.	Productive
*MONTE CARLO (H)	75	Indet.	VFN, ASC, St.	Flavorful
PATIO (H)	70	Dwarf	F, ASC	Pot-type
*SMALL FRY (H)	65	Det.	VFN, ASC, St.	Cherry
*TERRIFIC (H)	73	Det.	VFN, ASC, St.	Heavy producer
MANALUCIE (OP)	80	Indet.	F, ASC, St.	Old favorite
MARION (OP)	78	Indet.	F, St.	Old favorite
TINY TIM (OP)	60	Dwarf	ASC, St.	Cherry, pot-type
CATEGORY II				
BETTER BUSH (H)	72	Det.	VFN	Bush-type, long season
EARLY GIRL (H)	54	Indet.	—	Very early
GOLDEN BOY (H)	80	Indet.	ASC	Yellow, mild
CATEGORY III				
SWEET 100 (H)	65	Det.	—	Mild, cherry
SUPERSTEAK (H)	80	Indet.	VFN	Very large

*My favorites
Category I: Varieties I have grown successfully
Category II: Varieties recommended by reputation
Category III: Varieties which offer something new

KEY: (H) = Hybrid
(OP) = Open-pollinated
Indet. = Indeterminate (vine-type)
Det. = Determinate (bush-type)
V = Verticillium-resistant

F = Fusarium-resistant
N = Nematode-resistant
ASC = Resistant to Alternaria Stem Canker
St. = Resistant to Stemphylium
TMV = Resistant to Tobacco Mosaic Virus

Celebrity

Better Boy

Seedling tomato is set deeper than it was growing in the cell pack.

Well-grown tomato and eggplant seedlings ready for setting in the garden.

The author's post and wire method of training

follow garden rotation and other practices required to grow plants which are not resistant to these difficulties.

Almost every seed company has "the best" tomato variety to plant. Choosing your varieties is going to be confusing, at best. I repeat the admonition to go with what you have been successful with, leaving new ones for trial. One or two plants of a new variety which is "bigger, better, and four times longer" will be enough to convince you of the truth of the claims while at the same time involving minimum risk if the claims are not all you were led to expect.

There are some serious points to consider, however. If conditions in your garden have changed and you have run out of rotation areas, it may be necessary for you to replant in an old spot. You should certainly choose a VFN variety. If your space is more restricted than before, then a determinate variety would be best. There are some improved tomatoes with a shorter number of days until maturity, and so you might want to add to your garden for earlier harvests.

PLANTING AND GROWING

From a cultural standpoint, the tomato is a tender annual. It grows best when the weather is hot and, with the exception of a few varieties, the bloom will not set well when either the day or night temperature is below 50 degrees. It is a plant for the summer garden and should be set out after all danger of frost is past.

Since the tomato is a heavy feeder, the nutrient level must be kept uniform throughout the growing season. The balance of nutrients is also important; too high nitrogen amounts at fruit-setting time will reduce yields, yet too low nitrogen amounts in the early life of the plant will slow growth and prevent good yields. The first pre-plant fertilizing will not carry the tomato all the way through the season.

Tomatoes are rather indifferent to the pH of the soil. I have grown tomatoes in Georgia soil where the pH was 5.5 and in Egypt where it was 8.0. But tomatoes need calcium to help prevent a physiological disease referred to as blossom-end rot. Liming the soil each year is necessary to supply this needed calcium more than to change the pH.

There are many other cultural tips. I shall provide a series of notes to help you through some of the numerous problems facing the tomato grower on either a regular or rare basis.

Prepare tomato-growing areas at least six weeks ahead of planting. Work the ground deeply and, if you are planting on beds, prepare the beds ahead of time. During this preparation, work in 50 lbs. of ground limestone per thousand square feet.

Plant tomatoes after the air and soil are warming and there is no danger of even a light frost.

I plant tomatoes on a bed in an area of the garden that is evenly moist. Plant them neither in dry areas (unless you expect to water frequently) nor in soggy soil, which they do not like. I use the standard 30-inch wide bed with 3 feet between the edges of the bed.

There are two ways to plant. The first is to buy stocky transplants which are not too tender, or start your own plants ahead of time. It takes about six weeks from the time the seed are up until the plants are ready for the garden. The second way is to plug mix and plant the seeds directly in the spot where they will grow. This latter method is used mainly for large plantings.

Plug mixing means pre-germinating the seed in a sterile peat-light soil mixture. Simply mix 1/16 ounce of seed in a gallon of barely moist peat-light soil mixture and stir until the seeds are well distributed throughout the soil. Water the mixture some more until it is thoroughly moist but not soggy wet. Place the seed/soil mixture in a translucent plastic bag and leave it in a warm spot for several days. The warmer the spot, the fewer the number of days you need to leave it. Check occasionally for the first signs that the seed are starting to sprout. When this occurs, take the mixture to the garden for planting. Make a 2-inch-wide and 2-inch-deep hole at each point you want a plant. Fill up the hole with the mixture. When the plants have emerged from the ground, thin to a single plant per hole, transplanting any extras to holes where no seedlings came up. Take any extras to another area of the garden for more rows of tomatoes.

The advantage of plug-mixing is that it is quicker and more sure than direct seeding. The young seedlings also grow off extremely quickly and may catch up with older greenhouse or nursery plants which have a setback when first transplanted to the garden. Plug mixing works better for later plantings, rather than for early plantings.

I rework the beds, if necessary, right before planting to be sure they are loose and free from any spring weeds that have come up since the soil was prepared six weeks before. Now apply a pre-plant application of 10-10-10 fertilizer at the rate of about 2 lbs. per 25 feet of bed and work it into the entire bed.

I plant determinate varieties, like *Celebrity*, 30 inches apart and indeterminate varieties, like *Monte Carlo*, 36 inches apart. Closer plantings are also acceptable. In our fields in Egypt, we started with the wider spacings but eventually planted the determinates 18 inches apart and the indeterminates 28 inches. We gained considerable production this way. But in the home garden the close plantings may create an environment for leaf diseases and the need for more intensive spray programs, and so I have stayed with the wider spacings in my own garden.

Plant the seedlings deeper than they are growing in the pot or cell. Upon inspection you will notice two leaves on most seedlings which are long and entire. They bear little resemblance to the regular leaves. These are the seed leaves and indicate a good point up to which planting may occur. Tomatoes will root all along the part of the stem which is underground, so deep planting will increase the number of roots and lead to better growth.

Stake tomatoes when you are finished planting, because pushing the stakes into the ground later may stab and break some roots. The method of training your tomatoes is determined by your own desires and by the varieties you grow. Cages are fine. They are commercially available and also may be easily made from rolls of welded 6-foot-tall wire fencing. I have never liked cages because they are hard to cultivate around, and with so much foliage confined to such a small area, you must watch constantly for diseases and insects.

I have been very successful with two methods of training tomato plants. The first I used for over 10 years before moving to Egypt. After choosing the part of my garden where I planned always to grow tomatoes, I prepared the soil thoroughly with humus and manure. Then I set 6-foot treated posts at the end of each

A field of tomatoes in Egypt using the stake and string method of training.

The author teaching Filipinos the stake and string method of training tomatoes.

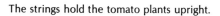

The strings hold the tomato plants upright.

The strong sucker just below the first bloom cluster should be left to make a wide, strong branching plant.

A mulch of grass clippings around tomatoes conserves moisture and keeps weed seeds from germinating.

row. The rows were 30 feet long, and the posts were set 2 feet in the ground in concrete for rigidity. Next, I placed into the post two heavy screws with large eyes, facing down the row, the first one 2 feet above the ground, and the second about 6 inches from the top of the post. I attached a turnbuckle to each eye, opened it wide, and attached a heavy No. 10 wire to the other end. I repeated the process on the post on the opposite end of the row. Now it was a simple matter to stretch the wire as tight as a drum by closing the turnbuckle. When I finished, I had two tight wires stretching the length of each row, one two feet off the ground, and the other almost 4 feet off the ground. I planted 10 plants per row, and as they grew, I tied the shoots to the wires with soft twine. When the crop began to get heavy I would place a lighter support post in the middle of each row to keep the wires from sagging too much under the heavy weight of the fruit.

The other method of training which I use now is the stake and string method. Place a heavy 6-foot 1 x 1 foot stake at the end of each row. Between the second and third plants, set another stake firmly in the ground. Continue setting stakes so that there are two plants between two stakes. As the tomato plants begin to grow, tie a heavy string on the stake at the end of the row and weave the string in and out to each stake down the row. This makes a cage of strings to hold the plants upright. The main advantage of the stake and string method of training is that it allows rotation around the garden year after year. This is not possible with the post and wire method.

Suckering

To sucker or not to sucker: That is the question which is argued *ad infinitum* among tomato growers. A sucker is a shoot which develops between a leaf and the stem. If allowed to develop, a sucker can produce fruit. The argument about a sucker's removal centers on the fact that on indeterminate varieties a main shoot will produce larger fruit than that produced on a shoot which originated as a sucker. Therefore, determinate varieties like *Celebrity* should not be suckered, while indeterminate varieties like *Monte Carlo* may or may not be. However, all tomatoes have a peculiar property; the first sucker below the first bloom cluster is capable of making a stem as strong as the main stem itself. Therefore, I always allow this sucker to develop and produce a wide, branching plant on both determinate and indeterminate types.

Suckering a plant is also an effective way to control its growth habit. By selective suckering, the gardener is able to alter the growth direction and shape of the plant.

The main advantage of suckering an indeterminate variety is that it increases the size of the fruit. If you are looking for prize winners, it is advisable to sucker, but if you want heavy production only, sucker the plant to make it grow as you want it to and to keep it under control.

Watering

The control of moisture on tomatoes is of utmost importance. The supply of moisture to the plant should be even, not alternately wet and dry. Cracking of the fruit is almost always related to improper watering or wet and dry conditions in nature.

Never water a lot, then stop for a while, and start watering again; there is great danger that way of having badly cracked fruit. On our desert farm where there was no rain, all the water was provided by irrigation. We found that watering too little or too much gave us immense cracking problems. In this dry environment, we had to have an exact schedule for each section of each field each day. If we watered a section in the morning of a given day, we had to water it every morning because skipping to the afternoon would cause cracking.

One of the best home garden tomato growers I know, Frank Player of Atlanta, devised a method of consistent watering which is worth passing on. Frank obtained a number of used 5-gallon plastic pails and drilled a lot of small holes around the bottom edge. Then he buried the pails, up to the lip, in the center of four plants. He kept these pails always filled with water and fertilizer. The solution slowly seeped into the ground at just the right rate and his tomatoes were constantly guaranteed ample water and nutrients.

In watering, never use sprinklers which wet the foliage. Tomatoes are susceptible to many blights and leaf spots which increase in intensity if the foliage is kept wet.

Fertilizing

Tomatoes must have an even supply of nutrients during the entire season. Alternately high and low periods of nutrients, like uneven watering, may cause cracking and poor fruit set. Frank Player's pails are a good way to keep the level of nutrients even. You may also use regularly, every three to four weeks, a light application of a 6-12-12 or 5-10-15 fertilizer, working it into the ground around the plants.

Often in the hottest weather of late summer, the vines may seem to be off-color and not growing well. This is because the root growth is not as active and the nutrients are not being taken into the plant. I add to my regular fertilizer program a foliar spray with a good soluble fertilizer to carry them through this poor growth time.

Mulching

I believe strongly in mulching my long-standing crops like tomatoes, peppers, and eggplants. This procedure helps keep the water supply to the plants more even and reduces the need for backbreaking weed control. Any good mulch is satisfactory, but my choice is dried grass clippings which I take from the lawn.

Harvesting

Like all vegetables, tomatoes should be kept cleanly harvested to encourage continued growth, bloom, and fruit set.

Harvest tomatoes at any stage after the entire fruit is pink, depending on how quickly you intend to use them. Harvesting in the full pink stage allows about a seven to ten-day shelf life under proper storage conditions.

Store tomatoes in a cool but not cold place, never under 50 degrees. Never refrigerate tomatoes until the final holding period after they are blood red. Storing pink tomatoes in the refrigerator will reduce considerably their taste and quality.

Sticky yellow strips hung among tomatoes will attract white flies away from the plants.

The white fly attacks tomatoes in mid to late summer.

Tomato Horn Worm

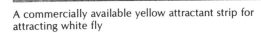

A commercially available yellow attractant strip for attracting white fly

Blossom End Rot is caused by a lack of calcium in the fruiting portion of the plant.

Tomato Fruit Worm

Yellowing of the leaves is caused by a Blight disease not a nutrient deficiency.

PROBLEMS

Tomatoes are affected by any number of insects and diseases, and you will need a regular spray or dust program to maintain healthy vigorous growth.

The worst diseases with which the home gardener must contend are Early Blight and Late Blight. In the South, Early Blight (Alternaria leaf spot) usually comes at the midpoint of summer and Late Blight in the earlier part of the season. Both can be extremely destructive if weather conditions are damp and muggy. Plants must be sprayed regularly when the first signs of the Late Blight disease occur as yellowing leaves toward the bottom of the plant, or when the first circular leaf spots of Early Blight are found. Dark linear spots on the stems are also symptoms of Early Blight.

Other diseases of some importance are: Alternaria Stem Canker, Stemphylium, Tobacco Mosaic Virus, and Bacterial Wilt. Of these, Tobacco Mosaic Virus is the most common problem and Bacterial Wilt the most destructive. The only control of either is removal of the affected plants from the garden and burning if that is allowed in your area. Garden cleanliness, including not smoking when handling tomato plants, is the best preventative against these two diseases.

The major insect pests of the foliage of the tomato are the tomato horn worm, tomato fruit worm, stem borers, and white fly. The white fly causes the most destruction to the plant. The horn worm is bad in the early growth stage and is pretty terrible to run across. One horn worm can defoliate a plant. A careful eye can spot these beasts and a good squash with the heel can control them. Fruit worms are destructive in the later part of the season. Both of these worms are easily killed by spraying or dusting with the Bacillus Thuringiensis, a very safe biological control.

Controlling white fly is a real problem. The population builds to monstrous proportion by late summer. I hang yellow boards painted with a soft sticky material throughout the tomato area. The white flies are attracted to the yellow color and get stuck. This method of control lasts only during the early and mid-season and is finally overpowered by the huge influx of white fly in later summer. Then you need to start a spray program specifically for this terrible insect. Check with your County Extension Service for the chemical recommended in your area.

The best way to control all these pests is to get a combination insecticide/fungicide spray and use it on a weekly basis. Prevention is the best way to have clean plants. When some problem occurs which is not being controlled by these regular cover sprays, check with your County Extension Service for specific advice.

I am providing a tomato problem solution chart that should help you in caring for your own plants.

TOMATO PROBLEMS AND SOLUTIONS

Symptom: Blossom-end turning black and corky

Cause: BLOSSOM-END ROT DISEASE
This is caused by a lack of calcium in the plant. Always lime your planting areas six weeks prior to planting. Water stress will also keep the

plants from taking up the calcium. Keep plants evenly moist. If blossom-end rot appears during the season, apply a prepared solution of calcium chloride as a spray.

Symptom: Black lesions on stem

Cause: BLIGHT
Spray immediately with Maneb or a combination insecticide-fungicide.

Symptom: Cracking

Cause: WATER AND NUTRIENT STRESS
Keep tomatoes evenly watered and fertilized. Mulching will also keep moisture level more even and help cracking problems as well as blossom-end rot problems (if calcium is in the soil).

Symptom: Drying of lower leaves

Cause: BLIGHT
Keep a cover spray of Maneb or a combination tomato spray on the plants. If this condition is not spreading up the plant, it may not be serious. It may also result from shading of lower leaves.

Symptom: Flowers drying up before setting

Cause: MANY CAUSES
Cold nights below 50 degrees or very hot days above 100 degrees may prevent pollination. Also, plants with heavy vine growth resulting from excessive nitrogen and plants in the near-wilt condition may drop their blossoms.

Symptom: Foliage eaten away, usually to a rib

Cause: TOMATO HORN WORM
Look for the ugly beast and squash that scoundrel! Spray or dust Bacillus Thuringiensis or use Sevin to kill the worm.

Symptom: Fruits with holes

Cause: TOMATO FRUIT WORM
Keep sprayed or dusted with Sevin, Bacillus Thuringiensis, or a combination tomato dust or spray.

Symptom: Fruits with dark spots or discolorations

Cause: BLIGHT
Keep on a cover spray of Maneb or a combination.

Symptom: Heavy vine growth and little fruit

Cause: FERTILIZER IMBALANCE
Too high nitrogen fertilizers may have been used. Use a 5-10-15 or 6-12-12 fertilizer for a period of time.

Symptom: Weak and spindly growth

Cause: SEVERAL CAUSES
This may be caused by too little direct sun, improper fertilizing, or soil that is too wet and soggy.

Symptom: Weak and spindly growth late in the summer

Black spots on the stem indicate an attack of Blight.

Late Blight usually begins with the dying of the lower leaves.

Just Right Hybrid Turnip

Purple Top White Globe Turnip

Southern Curled Mustard

Cause: FERTILIZER DEFICIENCY
Keep fertilizer on the plants through the season and keep evenly watered so that the plant can take up the nutrients from the soil.

Symptom: Wilting of the plant

Cause: MANY CAUSES
1. Fusarium and Verticillium Wilt will cause this problem and is usually first seen as tip wilt on hot days. Use resistant varieties.
2. Nematodes will cause symptoms similar to those above. Use resistant varieties.
3. Bacterial wilt will cause a more pronounced wilting. The stem right above the ground is generally soft and spongy. Since there is no cure, destroy the plant immediately before the disease spreads to other plants.
4. Stem borers will cause a wilting, but this is a rare condition. Regular cover sprays will generally control the adult before the eggs are laid.
5. Too much fertilizer will cause wilting, but this condition is generally accompanied by the browning of the edges of the leaves.

Symptom: Yellow spotting of the leaves

Cause: BLIGHT
This condition usually precedes the drying-up of the leaves. It is prevented by keeping a cover spray of Maneb or a combination spray on the plant.

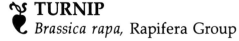 TURNIP
Brassica rapa, Rapifera Group

HISTORY

There is little doubt that the turnip has been with us for ages. This Old World vegetable has been written about from the early times and my old gardening books have all listed it. It seems to have originated from a wild plant which still grows in Scandinavia and throughout Eastern Europe.

There is some botanical difference between the turnip and the rutabaga (*Brassica Napus,* Napobrassica Group), which is a longer season plant and more hardy. However, since they are grown in much the same way as turnips, you will find rutabaga varieties listed with the turnips.

In the South, the turnip is grown mostly for the excellent salad greens; the root is only a secondary blessing. "Turnip salad" or, as many say, "turnip greens," has been a favorite food of Southerners from early colonial days. Many Southern restaurants made their reputations on the quality of their turnip greens. My grandfather insisted on eating at Ed Venable's restaurant in Atlanta at least once a week because it was the only place that really knew how to make corn bread and cook turnip greens.

To me, turnip greens with a proper pepper sauce is the only way to eat this plant, so don't be inviting me to a table filled with cooked turnip "bottoms." The earliest use of the bottom seems to have been for stock food which, in my opinion, is still the proper use. But to each his own, and here in the South the plant may be grown as well for one use as for the other.

FORMS AVAILABLE

There are some "bottomless" varieties which are produced for greens only and have been widely planted in the South for years along with mustard and rape. However, the new hybrid turnips produce large amounts of tender, delicious salad greens which may be the best inducement to the planting of a large root variety, even if you feed the bottoms to your pig (assuming, of course, that you have one).

TURNIP VARIETIES
15,000 Seeds per Ounce; 1 Ounce Plants 50 Feet of Row
Rutabagas Have 12,000 Seeds per Ounce

VARIETY	DAYS	ROOT COLOR	SPECIAL FEATURES
PURPLE TOP WHITE GLOBE	55	White/purple	Old favorite
ROYAL CROWN HYBRID	52	White/purple	Hybrid purple-top type
TOKYO CROSS HYBRID	35	White	May be left longer in soil
JUST RIGHT HYBRID	60	White	Grows large, good greens
SEVEN TOP SALAD	45	—	Slick leaves, good greens
AMERICAN PURPLE TOP RUTABAGA	90	Cream	Fall harvests only

PLANTING AND GROWING

Turnips are cool-weather plants and grow best in the spring and fall, producing equally well in either season. Plant the spring crop as soon as the hardest freezes have passed or, in most of our area, early to mid-March. Plant the fall crop when there is rain during the period from mid-August to mid-September.

I plant spring turnips on a 30-inch-wide bed which contains two rows twelve inches apart. I have also broadcast the seed on the bed for excellent results when growing for "salad" only.

Prior to planting, broadcast 10-10-10 fertilizer over the bed and work it in with a bow rake. Then open the tiny furrows and drill the seed. Thin the seedlings to a stand with the plants about 5 inches apart. I know some growers who thin several times, using the thinnings as salad greens for the table. The same spacing applies for the seed which are broadcast, and once again use the thinnings for salad greens.

I use the fall crop only for salad greens because it is better to plant in well-prepared, level soil during this time of possible rain shortages. In this tight soil the root seldom makes as well anyway. If you have the capability of irrigating, however, bed planting is still preferred if you are growing for the root crop (and you have a pig).

Keep turnips well-fertilized with a high nitrogen fertilizer, especially if you are growing them primarily for the greens.

Plant rutabagas in a similar way in drills on beds with the same fertilizing schedule, but since they are grown mainly for roots, use a 6-12-12 fertilizer for growth. Plant rutabagas for a fall crop only, but consider the long maturing time. Plant three months ahead of the first killing frost in your area. A spring crop is not suitable for the South due to the long maturing time.

Harvest turnip greens at any time when they are of sufficient size to gather. They do get tough and strong if left too long, especially after the weather is hot. You can harvest and freeze them for later use if you run into hot weather before you have gathered and eaten them.

After the harvest, wash them thoroughly to prevent gritty greens. My dear friend Celestine Sibley, an author of renown and my Sweet Apple neighbor, solves this problem by putting them in the washing machine, without soap, I am sure.

For you turnip bottom eaters, the reputed best size is two to three inches in diameter, though I wouldn't have much idea about this. Larger sizes are quite suitable for the pig.

PROBLEMS

Turnips have relatively few problems. Good bottoms develop only in loose soil and you need a high nitrogen fertilizer to have good tops for greens.

The only other problem is with aphids (plant lice) which attack in droves at the end of the spring season. These are easy to control with Malathion or dustings with Sevin, but be sure to wash the greens thoroughly if you have used a pesticide.

OTHER CROPS TO GROW

ENDIVE	KOHLRABI	PEANUTS
ESCAROLE	MISCELLANEOUS GREENS	RHUBARB
GOURDS	PARSLEY	SOYBEAN
KALE	PARSNIP	NEW ZEALAND SPINACH

MISCELLANEOUS GREENS

A number of plants grown exclusively for greens are harvested and brought to the table as a boiled dish. These are grown very much like turnips but add a different taste to the table. Some seedsmen even blend these together so that a delightful mixture of greens may be harvested and cooked at one time. There are also other plants whose tops afford a generous supply of delicious greens. Young radishes, amaranth spinach, and even dandelions may be harvested, boiled, and eaten. Beet greens may be the best of all.

Two plants which make excellent greens are mustard and rape. These two add a great deal to the garden.

Mustard (*Brassica juncea* var. *crispifolia*) provides excellent greens even into the early summer heat. The most commonly grown is the *Southern Curled Mustard*, with its attractive curled and plumed leaves.

Rape (*Brassica Napus*) has a smoother leaf, but makes an excellent spring, early summer, and fall green for the table.

Both of these greens, along with other frost-tolerant types, are sown at the same time as turnips after the heaviest freezes have passed. Plant them on a bed into which a 10-10-10 fertilizer has been worked. In the spring I use a standard 30-inch-wide bed made from thoroughly-tilled soil.

Broadcast the seed over the tilled bed and lightly rake the seed into the ground. Harvest the greens as needed after they reach sufficient size to cook. Mustard and rape will continue for several months. As long as they are growing rapidly, the leaves will be tender and may be taken. The only serious problem is the aphid which attacks as the weather warms. See Turnips for aphid control suggestions.

I plant the fall crop about the first of September but this time in thoroughly-prepared soil rather than on a bed. The fertilizing and culture are the same as in the spring. The fall crop will stand until hard freezes occur.

CHAPTER 3

PLANTING, GROWING, HARVESTING

We see now that vegetable gardening cannot be an impulse effort. Before getting to the moment of truth and planting, we must consider and do many things. We must choose the site for the garden, decide which crops to grow, make some sort of plan, and prepare the soil. This is not a one-afternoon job.

PLANTING FORMS: SEEDS, PLANTS, OR BULBS

The way you start your garden plantings will vary according to the crop you choose. With some crops the choice is easy, for there is only one way, but with others you may have one or more alternatives. Beans, for instance, are planted only from seed, while onions may be planted from seed, sets, or young plants. In the garden some crops are started from plants, while in commercial production this would never be done. I am always amazed to see cucumber, squash, and even watermelon plants available in plant stores and selling very well.

Another consideration is whether to produce your own plants, roots, or bulbs for setting in the garden or to purchase them from a plant outlet. There are no exact answers. If you are like me, starting seed for transplanting is a treasured part of the gardening experience. I enjoy producing plants ahead of time. But you may not have the inclination or facility to produce seedlings, so you will depend on friends or plant outlets for your young plants, bulbs, and roots.

The criterion to follow is your amount of time and space. A fifty-foot row of cucumbers will be a different matter from a ten-foot row. Why not raise or buy four or five plants of cucumbers rather than plant a whole pack of seed?

The serious gardener may run into problems from the lack of choice varieties available as plants in the nursery or plant shop. It is a hard proposition to find the right variety of seed in the seed rack, much less the best variety on the plant tables. Also, at the time you want to plant, the best plants may not be available. So why not start ahead of time and grow your own?

The following table will help you choose among the available alternatives—seeds, bulbs, plants, roots, or "eyes."

PLANTING FORMS

CROP	SEED	PLANTS	BULB	ROOT	DIVISION	SPECIAL FEATURES
ARTICHOKE, GLOBE	X				XX	side shoots
ARTICHOKE JERUSALEM				X		
ASPARAGUS	X			XX		seed take some years
BEAN	XX					
BEET	XX					
BROCCOLI*	X	XX				transplants
BRUSSELS SPROUT*	X	XX				transplants
CABBAGE*	X	XX				transplants
CANTALOUPE	XX	X				plants for a few
CARROT	XX					
CAULIFLOWER*	X	XX				transplants
CELERIAC*	X	XX				transplants
CELERY*	X	XX				transplants
COLLARD	XX	X				
CORN	XX					
COWPEA	XX					
CRESS*	X	XX				transplants
CUCUMBER	XX	X				plants for a few
EGGPLANT*	X	XX				transplants
ENDIVE*	XX	X				plants for a few
ENGLISH PEA	XX					

CROP	SEED	PLANTS	BULB	ROOT	DIVISION	SPECIAL FEATURES
ESCAROLE	XX	X				like endive
GARLIC			XX			"cloves" of bulbs
GOURD	XX					
HONEYDEW	XX	X				plants for a few
KALE	XX	X				
KOHLRABI*	X	XX				transplants
LEEK	X	XX				transplants
LETTUCE*	XX	XX				use both
OKRA	XX					
ONION**	X	XX	XX			
PARSLEY*	X	XX				seeds are slow
PARSNIP	XX					
PEANUT	XX					
PEPPER***	X	XX				transplants or nursery plants
POTATO, IRISH					eyes	side buds of tuber
POTATO, SWEET		XX				"slips"
PUMPKIN	XX					
RADISH	XX					
RHUBARB				XX		
RUTABAGA	XX					
SALSIFY	XX			X		mostly from seeds for first crop
SHALLOT			XX			
SOYBEAN	XX					
SPINACH	XX					
SPINACH, NEW ZEALAND	XX					
SQUASH	XX	X				plants for a few
SWISS CHARD	XX					
TOMATO****	X	XX				most types available in nurseries
TURNIP	XX					
WATERMELON	XX	X				

X = Alternative Form   XX = Common Form

*Start these from seed yourself to insure getting the best varieties. Nursery selections are generally limited.

**Onions are tricky to start from seed, but this may be necessary for specific varieties. Onion "sets" are small bulbs generally grown for green onions, while plants are generally used for large bulbous crops.

***Though pepper plants are generally available, play it safe with specific varieties and start them yourself.

****Wide selections of tomato plants are generally available in nurseries, but start the new, and unique varieties from seed.

The main considerations for choosing among these different types is availability and quality. The quality of your favorite nursery or plant shop will determine, in many cases, whether you start plants yourself from seed or wait to buy them already growing. Certainly it is easier to pop into a plant supplier for a few tomato and pepper plants than to go to the trouble and expense of starting them in February and looking after them for such a long period of time. But can you find good disease-free plants in your supplier's shop at just the time you want them? Can you find that new variety or an old favorite that is just right for you? These are questions only you can answer.

I have found over many years that cabbage, collard, onions (sets and plants), tomato, pepper, eggplant, both types of potatoes, and the permanent crops like Jerusalem artichoke, asparagus, horseradish, and rhubarb can be found dependably in most plant outlets. Most others are best started yourself.

SELECTING NURSERY SEEDLINGS

No matter how wide the variety list is at your plant outlet, take extreme care in picking out the plants. Biggest is seldom best. Young succulent plants are going to take hold and grow off faster than tough, old plants. A young, vigorous tomato, pepper, or eggplant grown in a two-inch pot may well produce quicker than a tough oldster growing in a gallon container, and the young plant is a lot less expensive.

Never buy squash or melons which have already begun to run. The runners are too easy to break, and the plants may sit in the garden for weeks before starting to grow rapidly. An ideal transplanting size for squash and melons is after the true leaves have reached full size and before the plants fall over and start running.

Irish potatoes should be firm; asparagus roots should not be shriveled, and onion sets should have no rot or foul smell. Always inspect tomato plants for spots on the stems or leaves which might indicate the early stages of blight.

Pay attention to the container in which the small plant has been grown. The new cell packs are an ideal way to handle young seedlings. We used this method to plant hundreds of acres of tomatoes, melons, broccoli, peppers, and squash on our commercial farm in Egypt with virtually no loss. The cell pack allows the planter to handle many small plants without the breaking which occurs when setting out individually-grown plants. But cell packs can accommodate fast-growing vegetable seedlings for only a short time. Never buy cell pack plants that are off-color or too tall. The roots will be so compacted in the cell that they will have difficulty starting good, fast growth.

Be careful when buying seedlings in pressed peat or fiber pots. These are hard to keep wet enough for the roots to penetrate and continue penetrating. It is a good idea to remove these pots before planting rather than planting pot and all, as suggested.

Joemarie Galve planting seed in the Philippines.

STARTING PLANTS FROM SEED

I take great delight in producing my own plants from seed. First, I am assured of having the exact variety of plant I want because, by starting ahead, I can search stores and catalogs for the varieties and order when necessary. Second, I have a greater inducement to get the garden ready well ahead of time so that as soon as the weather is right I can go to the garden with my young plants. Third, I have much greater flexibility since I do not need to search for the right variety. Finally, it is just plain fun to grow your own.

On a very hot day in the Philippines, I was showing our best seed planter, Joemarie Galve, how to seed lettuce in a seed bed. He carefully dropped each seed at its proper spacing, and I followed him in the row, carefully covering the seed. As I covered each part of the row, I would pat the planted row and call out, "Grow, plants, grow!" Joemarie lit up with a huge smile each time I called out. Soon he and all the other seed planters were doing the same thing. All through the seed bed area there was a constant call of "Grow, plants, grow!" in English, a language quite foreign to these Ilonggo-speaking people. The remarkable result was our excellent germination. They, like most of us, are awed by the miracle of those tiny seeds growing and becoming something wonderful.

I have often said that it takes faith to believe a tiny seed will produce a head of lettuce. I know that planting tiny seeds and expecting beautiful plants to result may be just as foreign to many of you as it was to Joemarie and our other Filipino seed planters. But to me, with my background in the seed business, it is the most natural and the best way to get started gardening.

I like to plant all kinds of seeds. Tree seeds, shrub seeds, vegetable seeds, and flower seeds show up in my pockets all the time. Sometimes this causes problems for Betsy, like the time she was doing the wash and found an M & M look-alike object in my pocket. She popped it in her mouth expecting a delicious chocolate taste, only to bite into a seed as bitter as gall. She said it served her right, trying to steal my M & M.

Starting plants from seeds is a creative adventure, and a very practical way to have a more diversified garden. It is also economical. One pack of seeds can produce an abundance of plants at a very small cost in comparison with "store-bought" plants.

There are two ways to start plants from seeds. The first way is the time-honored method of direct seeding. Farmers plant beans, corn, grain, and many other crops by preparing the land, making rows, dropping the seeds in the row, and covering them. You can do this by hand in small areas or by machine in large areas. Many crops are best planted in this manner. In the vegetable garden especially, this is the best way to start beans, peas, corn, melons, squash, okra, and other large-seeded vegetables, many of which do not transplant well because of the nature of their root systems.

Direct seeding is fine for large-seeded vegetables and flowers.

A plastic seed tray is ideal for starting seeds ahead of time and for starting small seeds.

Tomatoes and peppers are best started inside while the weather outside is still cold. They will be ready to set in the garden when warm weather arrives.

The second way is by seeding in beds, trays, cells, or pots and then transplanting to the garden when the seedlings are of a tough enough size to be handled easily. Since direct seeding into the garden is covered by the discussions on vegetables, I will explain the second way of seeding for transplanting here.

I grew up calling this practice "starting seeds ahead of time," which is an appropriate term since that is exactly what the practice calls for. You are starting seeds before you will be needing the plants for the garden.

Practically speaking, this gives you a jump on the season. You can start seeds in a warm place inside while the weather is still freezing outside, and your plants will be ready to put out when the weather is right.

This is extremely important for a number of crops which suffer in our hot climate, especially those cool-weather crops like broccoli, cabbage, cauliflower, and lettuce which need to mature before hot weather comes.

Certain other plants like tomatoes, eggplants, and peppers just do better when they are transplanted. This practice assures stronger, stockier plants to withstand the trials and tribulations of early growth.

There are a number of reasons why I start plants from seeds for my garden:

- The plants will be available when I want them.
- I can obtain a wider variety of plants from seed than I can generally find in plant outlets because they are not commercially grown as plants.
- The plants will be ready for setting in the garden earlier than they are available in plant outlets.
- It is far less expensive raising plants from seed than buying the plants themselves.
- Some types of plants produce extraordinarily small seeds which are difficult to germinate and grow unless they are nurtured in the controlled environment of a seed tray or seedling pot.
- Some types of plants just develop more quickly and are stronger when they are started in a tray and transplanted.

WHAT YOU NEED TO START SEED AHEAD

Like most gardening, starting seeds ahead can be simple or complex, depending on the gardener's wishes. It may include simply a seed tray or a pot and a homemade growth chamber; it may be as complex as having a greenhouse with a controlled temperature. The principles are the same:

- A proper place to start seedlings
- A correct and sterile soil mixture
- A tray or pot deep enough to allow good root growth
- Ample light
- A way to water with a fine stream
- A temperature which is warm but not too hot, especially at night

You can alter and refine each of these principles to fit your own facilities if you respect the principles.

A Place To Start Seeds

A greenhouse is ideal for starting seeds ahead of time because its environment can be controlled for optimum seedling development. Years ago I built an A-frame greenhouse out of treated wood and rigid plastic for just under $100. It is not the prettiest greenhouse in the world, but it has served us admirably for over 15 years. In it I grow all my seedlings with little effort. A homemade or "store-bought" greenhouse adds so much to a gardener's joy that I highly recommend getting one if it fits into your lifestyle. However, there are alternatives for the many people who may not find a greenhouse possible.

A cold frame is a simple box-like structure with a transparent top which may be opened to prevent heat build-up. If possible, it should face south so that it can receive the warm winter sun. The bottom, where the

The author designed and built this "A" frame greenhouse at very little cost. It has lasted for over 15 years.

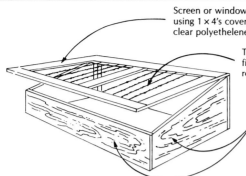

Screen or window sash. May be constructed using 1 x 4's covered with 4 mil or 6 mil clear polyethelene film of clear fiberglass

Twisted wire to support polyethelene film (if used). Fiberglass does not require support.

Construct cold frame box from 2-inch thick cedar, redwood or pressure treated timbers. Exterior plywood (3/4" thick) may be used, but should be treated to prevent decay.

Cold frame box has no bottom. Front should be about 8 to 10 inches above ground. Back should be 14 to 18 inches above ground. Length of box should be approximately 6 feet.

Provide means of supporting top in open position to allow for proper ventilation. If desired, a thermal hinge may be installed to automatically open the top at 72° and close it at 68°.

A simple cold frame which was designed by an Atlanta gardener.

Courtesy: The Southern Garden Club Newsletter; Published by Don Hastings, Sr.

seed pots or trays are placed, should be 8 to 12 inches below ground level to preserve heat during the cold nights. If you add a heating cable for the soil, it becomes a hotbed instead of a cold frame. This is important when starting seeds in the winter because they take very warm temperatures to germinate.

You can start seeds also in trays in a bright, sunny window of the house or in a warm solarium room. But you must take great care to provide extra air moisture because the humidity inside a house is very low when the furnace is on. You can add moisture with a cold air vaporizer, or by placing the pots or trays in a simple growth chamber which you can make easily from a seed flat, coathangers, and a plastic dry cleaning bag.

After planting your tray, just straighten out 3 or 4 coathangers and bend each of them into a semi-circle. Insert the ends of the coathanger into the sides of the tray as if they were the ribs of a covered wagon. Then slip

A simple growth chamber can be made by unhooking a coat-hanger and using it as a frame for a tent made by slipping the tray into a plastic cloths bag.

131

A peat-light, soilless mixture of ground bark, peatmoss, perlite, and vermiculite

the whole tray with its ribs into a plastic dry cleaning bag and close it up with a twist tie. There you have a simple homemade growth chamber.

The simplest structure for starting a few seeds is an 8-inch pot filled with a good seeding mixture and covered with a piece of cling-wrap plastic.

Soil Mixture

The quality of the soil is the quickest way for you to succeed or fail. If you do not have a good mixture in which to start seeds, you will have poor results.

Use a very light, sterile potting mixture. A peat-light mixture drains well, releases excess moisture, and has the ability to retain enough moisture for good germination. The mixture should be sterile to prevent "damping off" or other soil fungus problems.

Seed Trays and Pots

The structure which holds the soil should be of sufficient size to handle easily. It should be deep enough to hold ample soil for good root development of the seedlings. I find that a seed tray about 3 to 4 inches deep is ideal. The tray must have drain holes or spaces in the bottom to allow excess moisture to move out.

Plastic seed trays are readily available from plant stores, where they are used as carriers for small potted plants and generally thrown away after the plants have been sold. If the tray does not have drainage holes, heat an ice pick until it is red hot and punch a number of holes in the bottom of the tray.

Many growers will start seeds in a tray or "seed flat" and transplant them into pots or cell trays. I find this an excellent practice because transplanting will make most seedlings stronger and stockier. Seeding directly into the cell tray or small pots is all right for some difficult-to-transplant crops like lettuce and for large-seeded vegetables like asparagus.

Seed flats are easy to build and many "knocked-down" versions are available commercially. When making your own, be sure that the base slats are spaced about 1/8-inch apart to allow good drainage. In the Philippines I ordered some seed flats to be made. Joemarie's father produced some beautiful flats which I could hardly lift. To my astonishment I found they were made of solid mahogany, a cheap native wood which is readily available there. Can you imagine having seed flats made of one of the most beautiful woods in the world?

You can start small quantities of seed in a 6 or 8-inch pot. Fill the pot with a good peat-light mixture which you have first thoroughly dampened. Leave about an inch between the top of the soil and the edge of the pot. After seeding, place a piece of clear plastic cling-wrap over the top to make it like a little greenhouse.

Plastic seed trays, plastic cell packs, and plastic pots are all ideal for starting seeds ahead of time.

For a few seeds, a 6- or 8-inch pot is ideal.

Seed trays should have holes in the bottom for good drainage.

Seed flats in the Philippines were made from native mahogany, one of the world's most beautiful woods.

133

Light for Seedlings

Light is extremely critical for germinating seeds. Seedlings which develop in too little light will be weak and spindly; when they are transplanted, they will suffer badly from the increased light they find in the open garden. So for best results, place your trays or pots in a bright, sunny place where they will receive high-quality light most of the day.

Watering Seedlings

Before planting your seeds, be sure that the medium is thoroughly watered. After planting the seeds, place a piece of plastic over the tray or pot, even in a greenhouse, to keep from having to water again before germination. Many extremely small seeds must be planted very shallowly. You should water these only when absolutely necessary before the seeds germinate, because many seeds can be washed completely out of the medium. However, if you ever allow the medium to dry out, you may lose your germination. If you must water, buy a fog-mist nozzle for the hose and use its very fine spray to keep the surface from drying out.

After germination, be very careful when watering so that the young seedlings are not bent over and plastered to the top layer of the soil.

Growth Temperature

Most seedlings are best grown at a day temperature of around 70 degrees F. and a night temperature of about 55–60 degrees F. The night temperature is more critical than the daytime temperature. Too-high temperatures during night hours will cause spindly growth.

This is all general information; you will find that each seed type will vary somewhat. Cool-weather plants like cabbage and hardy perennial flowers should be grown at cooler temperatures in both day and night. Hot-weather vegetables like pepper and eggplant, and flowers like zinnias, will require warmer daytime temperatures, but do not let the nighttime temperature rise above 60 degrees F.

SEEDING

Once you understand what you need, it's time for you to get started. Have all your materials—growing structures, seed flats, trays or pots, hose nozzles, plastic covering, soil mixture, seeds, and pot labels—ready when you start. Then proceed step by step until you have all the seeds planted for that time, as follows:

1. Place the soil mixture in a large container and wet it thoroughly. Allow all the excess moisture to drain out before filling your flats, trays, or pots.
2. Fill your growing containers with the mixture and tamp the soil to firm it. The top of the soil surface should be at least 1/2-inch below the edge of the tray or 1 inch below the edge of a pot. I have found that

Fill seed tray with a thoroughly moistened peat-light mixture, firm with a wood block and open rows across tray with a straight edge.

After seeding each variety, be sure and mark each with the variety name and date planted. Labels read front to back, left to right.

cutting a 2 × 4 the width of my flats for use in tamping down the soil works beautifully.

3. Determine how deeply each type of seed should be planted. The seed packet will tell you. It is most important to follow these directions strictly.

4. Make the rows across the tray or flat. For my own planting, I have cut a wooden ruler which fits easily across my flats. With the edge of the ruler, I press into the soil to make a groove at the right depth for the seed to be planted. I try to plant all the seeds which need the same planting depth together in the flat so that I can make a number of rows at one time.

5. Now I make labels for all the seeds I am planting that day. I put the name and date planted on each label.

6. Split open the package of seed and pour a small number of seeds into the palm of your hand. Start seeding the rows on the extreme left side of the flat as you face it. Seed front to back, left to right. With your working hand, carefully take the seed from your palm and place in the row. Pour more seed from the pack as needed. Sow seeds thinly. Seedlings will be difficult to transplant if their roots grow together.

7. When you finish a variety, pinch the row closed with your fingers.

8. Label the row before you go on because it's hard to remember afterward where and what you planted. The rules of labeling are strict.

Always place labels front to back, left to right, and since this is the way you planted, it becomes easy to remember.

9. After you have planted all the rows, take your block of wood and tamp the soil to firm it.
10. At this point, I scatter a fine layer of milled sphagnum moss over the surface to help control damp-off and to prevent the surface from drying.
11. Next, if you have made a growth chamber, slip the tray inside it. If you don't have one, place a piece of clear plastic cling-wrap over the top of the tray.
12. Place the tray in the spot where you will grow your seedlings.
13. Seeding in a pot is similar, with the following exceptions:
    • Seed only one type or variety in a pot.
    • Instead of making rows, place the seed on the surface and cover with damp soil to the required depth.
    • Place one label per pot.
    • Cover the top of the pot with cling-wrap.
14. Watch your trays or pots daily. Do not let the surface dry out. Water with a mist spray if necessary.
15. If fungus appears on the surface or on the germinating seedlings, take off the cling-wrap or open up the growth chamber and allow it to dry out a bit.

TRANSPLANTING

One of the secrets of having good plants for the garden is transplanting properly. Some gardeners allow the seedlings to grow in the flat until ready to put outside in the garden. I find this a bit rough on the plant, and the loss rate may be unacceptable. Therefore I transplant from the seed flat into a small pot or cell pack to develop the seedlings further before time to put them in the garden. Here is how I do it:

1. Transplant after the true leaves (not the seed leaves, which look different) have developed.
2. Transplant when the seedling is strong enough to handle without breaking.
3. Transplant into a pot or cell which is neither too large nor too small. I like a 3-inch pot or a 2-inch cell for almost all seedlings.
4. Use the same peat-light mixture that you used in the seed flat or seeding pot.
5. Carefully take up a few seedlings from the row in the flat. I use an old kitchen spoon as a trowel.
6. Make a deep hole in the center of the pot or cell with your index finger.
7. Carefully separate a seedling from the group you lifted from the flat or pot and place it in the hole. You will notice that the soil level is way up the stem. Do not cover any leaves. This is one of the few times in gardening when you bury a stem.

Plants should have their true leaves, be tough and large enough to handle without breaking before they are removed from the seedling tray.

Do not try to transplant seedlings before they grow their true leaves.

Plastic cell packs are ideal for growing transplanted seedlings.

An old kitchen spoon is ideal for lifting seedlings out of the tray without breaking them.

Make a hole in the center of the pot into which you put the seedling.

8. Either label each pot or cell, or place them in rows so that the label in the first pot of each group adheres to our label rule, "Read front to back, left to right."
9. Grow in bright, sunny light at temperatures like those for the germinating seedlings.
10. You will have to fertilize them to develop strong plants suitable for setting in the garden. Use a balanced soluble fertilizer in a mild liquid solution as needed to maintain rich color and good growth.
11. Transplant your plants into the garden when the roots have matted against the sides of the pot or cell and the plants are tough enough to handle.
12. In the early spring, I like to set my transplants outside in the sun to acclimate them. Be careful, however, not to let frost or extreme cold hurt them. Move them inside on cold nights.

This Filipino worker is doing his transplanting job well.

The author showing how to transplant tomatoes into the field in the Philippines.

13. Keep transplants watered well. Wilting will retard their development. Water thoroughly as the surface begins to dry out.
14. Don't let the plants fall over. Watering them too heavily or leaving them too long before transplanting may make the tops too large to stand up.

TIMING OF SEEDLING PRODUCTION

It is important to start seedlings at the right time so they will be at the right size to set in the garden at the best planting time. There are no exact rules to help you, because temperature, day length, sunny days, and the quality of light where they are grown will cause variations in the development rate of your seedlings. But there are some general rules which will help you determine when to start them. In the winter, it will take the seeds of cool-weather crops about 8 weeks to produce a plant ready for setting out. It will take the seeds of hot-weather crops about 8 weeks if they are seeded before the spring equinox, and about 6 weeks if they are seeded after the spring equinox. Pepper and eggplant seeds will take one to two weeks longer than tomatoes.

This timing starts from when the seed germinates, and there is a tremendous variation in that. Tomatoes and lettuce may appear in a few days; eggplant may take a week. You will soon learn how long it takes each crop to be ready. Remember that you marked the planting date on each label. If you keep good notes, you can improve your timing each year.

PLANTING YOUR CROPS

Those of us who have been gardening awhile find it hard to understand the dilemma which the new gardener faces. Suddenly, on a warm, sunny April afternoon the new gardener races to the store for a few plants, having in mind to start a garden. But too often reality rears its head and the garden project is relegated to projects never finished.

By the time planting day arrives, much forethought and preparation needs to have been completed. One of the best admonitions I have ever seen was on a large sticker on the cold air vaporizer we purchased after our first son was born. It read simply:

"HONESTLY, NOW, HAVE YOU READ THE INSTRUCTIONS?"

In other words, be prepared when you start! Success comes from a combination of many factors leading up to planting as well as how the crops are planted and cared for later on.

SUPPLIES AND MATERIALS

With those exhortations aside, we can begin to talk about planting. You need only a few things in addition to all the planning you've done:
- The garden plan
- Seeds and/or plants
- A Warren hoe. This is the sharp-pointed hoe I mentioned before.

An eight-inch flower pot makes an excellent fertilizer distributor.

Use a string to keep rows straight.

- Fertilizer. For winter crops, I prefer a 5-10-15 formula. For summer crops, I prefer a 10-10-10 formula.
- A large bucket into which you have poured your fertilizer (so you won't have to struggle with a 40- or 50-lb. bag)
- A 6 or 8-inch flower pot with a single drain hole
- A long piece of cord to keep the rows straight and two stakes, one for each end of the row
- Large plant stakes to mark the rows with the names of the crops. You can omit these if you promise to mark what you have planted on your paper plan.

Now you can begin planting!

PLANTING METHODS

I have talked about three methods of growing vegetables in the discussion of vegetable types and in the section on preparing to plant: furrows, hills and beds. There is a fourth method called broadcasting, which is used when spacing is not important. After the soil is thoroughly prepared, scatter the seed evenly over the area and rake it into the ground.

The method of planting is determined by what you plant and when the crop is to be grown. Refer to individual vegetable types for information as to which method to use at each planting season. Don't be afraid to change your method of planting from time to time. Each garden is different and you should let your own conditions dictate how you plant. My methods are for my garden and provide a good place for the beginner to start.

Planting in Furrows

Planting in furrows is the most common method. For large-seeded crops like beans or corn, we will open a straight furrow, using the pointed hoe and a string to keep it straight. Open the furrow about 4 inches deep. Now place your finger under the drain hole and fill the flower pot with fertilizer. Starting at the beginning of the furrow, release your finger and walk

Using the string as a guide, open a 4-inch deep furrow with a pointed hoe.

Fill the pot with fertilizer keeping your finger under the drain hole until you reach the furrow.

At the beginning of the furrow, take away your finger to allow the fertilizer to meter into the furrow as you walk quickly down the row.

Work the fertilizer into the bottom of the furrow, drawing loose soil into the furrow until the proper planting depth is attained.

Drop the large seeds into the furrow by hand.

Seed thicker than the proper spacing for the type, and thin to a stand.

quickly down the row, allowing the fertilizer to meter into the furrow as you go. At the end of the row, stop the fertilizer by placing your finger under the drain. Go to the next furrow and repeat the procedure.

Once you have applied the fertilizer, take the pointed hoe and work it into the furrow, at the same time drawing soil from the side into the furrow until the proper planting depth for the seed has been reached. Use the same method when planting in furrows in the ground or in beds.

You can plant the seed in any number of ways. Almost every gardener devises his own method of distributing the seed into the furrow. You can buy a wheel planter, or use a hand-held tube which can be adjusted to allow individual seeds to fall out, or you can plant by hand. Frankly, I always plant by hand; it just seems faster and easier. No matter how you do it, the object is to place seed in the furrow spaced evenly so that you can thin the plants later on. Too few seeds may cause skips when some seeds do not germinate, and too many seeds make thinning a real chore.

After seeding, take the pointed hoe and draw soil over the seeds until the furrow is filled. After each row has been planted, write the name of the vegetable and the variety on the row stake and mark the row, or write the name on your planting chart. DON'T FORGET! Let me warn you: As soon as the seed are covered and the garden is planted, it is hard to remember what went where.

Plant very fine-seeded vegetables in a similar way except make the furrow extremely shallow. I plant lettuce, carrots, etc., by putting the fertilizer on the bed and working it in before opening the tiny furrow. The

Carefully seeding lettuce into a slight furrow in the Philippines.

A hill is made by drawing loose soil into and above the furrow at an interval suited to the crop.

Seed five or six seeds per hill.

Thin to two or three strong plants.

rest of the procedure is the same. This is called planting in drills because there is no effort to space the seed. The seed are allowed to flow continuously into the furrow. You can have some spacing by adjusting the rate of flow. There are implements which "drill" seed in the ground and cover the seed at the same time. These planters are widely used in commercial planting, but I have never seen any for the home garden.

Planting in Hills

I do hill planting in a similar way. First, I open a furrow and fertilize as above. Then, with the pointed hoe, I form the hills over the furrow by drawing surrounding soil into and on top of the furrow. Plant the seed carefully in the hill. Drop several seed on the hill (I usually use about 5 seed per hill), and with your finger poke them into the hill one by one. Then draw a little more soil onto the hill to fill the poked holes. Another method of hill planting is to draw soil over the furrow until the hill is almost the height that you want it. Drop the seed on the hill and cover them with the proper amount of soil for the correct planting depth. The hill will then be at the correct height.

Planting in Beds

Bed planting is becoming increasingly popular for spring gardens in the South. Growing plants on beds allows the heavy spring rains to drain

Planting on well prepared beds allows good drainage when rainfall is high.

Very fine seeds of crops like mustard or turnips for greens may be broadcast over a bed which has been finely raked.

away from the seedlings, preventing cold, wet conditions which would inhibit growth. Bed planting also allows root crops to develop in loose soil which does not become compacted in hot, dryer weather.

A bed is a wide ridge that is made over the row either by hand or with an implement like a hiller. Soil from the middle is drawn up over the row. The width of the bed is determined by the crop to be grown, but is usually from 24–36 inches wide.

Setting plants, bulbs, roots, and tubers in a bed is not hard, provided the soil is prepared well. Open the furrow and fertilize as you did before. After working in the fertilizer, place the plants or bulbs in the furrow at the proper spacing. Carefully draw the proper amount of soil into the furrow to cover the plants at the right depth.

FINAL TOUCHES

After planting each row, remember to write on your garden plan the name of the variety, the date planted, and any other information you feel will be useful in the future. You may wish to record which fertilizer formula you used and other information such as weather, soil moisture, and the source of the seed or plants.

You will learn the best methods of planting in your garden as the seasons pass. Don't be afraid to deviate from my suggestions. Each of us can become an expert on his own piece of land, just as each new season makes a novice out of the most experienced gardener as strange, unforeseen things happen and nature provides new challenges.

GROWING YOUR CROPS

I have known vegetable growers who spent so much time, study, and effort starting the crops that growing them became an anticlimax, and they never produced satisfactory vegetables for harvest. In fact, a commercial grower I knew had this problem. In the whole time I knew him, he never produced even one satisfactory crop. As soon as the vegetables should have been at the peak of harvest, he was ready to plow them up since they "weren't going to make."

This is an easy trap to fall into because there is so much exhilaration in the steps leading up to the time the crop begins to grow. Often, interest falls away when the crop is in the long growing period before harvest. I like to watch plants grow! Sometimes I think that I stare them to death. Growing the crop is the "meat" of vegetable gardening for me, and the harvest is the "dessert."

BASIC GROWTH REQUIREMENTS

In my university days, my freshman botany professor always stressed the basics. I think that is the best way to talk about growing vegetables. Plants need only a few basic things to grow. Your application of these basics determines whether the vegetables are going to produce well or not. The basics are heat, light, water, carbon dioxide, oxygen, nutrients, and a proper growing medium.

Heat Requirement

Heat is necessary to make the plant's chemical processes work. Of course, each type of plant requires a different amount of heat. As I have shown, lettuce may be grown in colder temperatures than eggplant. English peas will bloom and produce in temperatures where tomato blossoms will not pollinate. Since it is almost impossible to change the temperature in the garden, the gardener accommodates himself to this requirement by choosing the correct season to grow each crop.

Light Requirement

Light requirements also vary from plant species to species. Thus we choose the garden location which has the proper light for each type of vegetable we are going to grow.

Water Requirement

Water is essential for all plants. Once again we are dependent, to a large extent, upon nature to provide the proper water for the plants we are growing. However, as I have described in the section on types of vegetables, the garden location will help lessen your dependence on nature. Some crops, like okra, will produce under drier conditions than tomatoes will and may be planted in the areas of the garden which dry out more quickly. Water, however, can affect growth adversely when there is too much in the soil, as we will see when we look at the growing medium. You may be able to irrigate or water the garden. If you can, always do it properly and carefully because improper watering can harm as much as it can help. Water thoroughly each time you feel it is necessary. Moisture meters may be of some help, but I have seen these be more hindrance than help when used improperly. The probe must be set in the right place inside the feeder root zone and the readings must be interpreted properly.

I check my soil moisture with a pointed hoe by opening up a few inches of the area to see if there is any moist soil under the surface. Tip-wilting of the plants in the late afternoon also indicates a lack of water.

I prefer furrow irrigation or trickle (drip) irrigation for vegetables. This puts the water in the root area without wetting the foliage; wet foliage invites insect and disease problems.

Like my friend Frank Player, who buries 5-gallon plastic buckets with holes in the sides in his garden, you will probably devise your own system. Remember: Too little water is bad; too much is bad. Frequent shallow watering may be disastrous, while infrequent deep watering will keep plants growing well.

Carbon Dioxide and Oxygen Requirement

Because of the process of photosynthesis in which plants take water and carbon dioxide and chemically turn it into sugar, we overlook their need for oxygen. Oxygen is required as the plant metabolizes its sugars and starches for growth. It is true, though somewhat simplistic, that plants use carbon dioxide and give off oxygen in their basic processes. However, plants in the process of metabolism need oxygen to generate growth. The roots are particularly sensitive to the lack of proper oxygen in the soil, which is a fact we will look at once again when we study the medium for growing. Though some greenhouse operators have had success with enriched air containing higher levels of oxygen and carbon dioxide, the gardener must depend on nature for these items necessary for growth.

Nutrient Requirement

Nutrients are the minerals which the plant requires to produce. Nitrogen, phosphorous, and potash are the main ones, though many others are needed in very tiny quantities. These minor or trace elements may make or break your crop.

Fertilizer is *not* food for the plant, despite the labels on many bags of garden fertilizer which state that they are complete "plant foods." These minerals are necessary for plant growth, but they do not feed the plant. They are merely absorbed into the plant, where they provide the elements for growth to take place. The food is produced by the plant itself in the miraculous process of photosynthesis. It is wise to buy a garden fertilizer with the minor or trace elements listed so that these micro-nutrients will always be in the soil when needed.

Fertilizer nutrients are necessary to grow good crops.

The chemical symbols for the macro-nutrients nitrogen, phosphorus, and potash are those letters always seen on a bag of fertilizer, N,P,K. They are always listed in that order so that when you see a 10-10-10 fertilizer you know there is 10 percent nitrogen, 10 percent phosphorus, and 10 percent potash. This analysis of the fertilizer is required by law on each bag. Minor elements are not required by percentage, but I have more trust in the product when the minor elements are also listed on the bag with the percentage of each.

Generally speaking, nitrogen is for the green areas of the plant, phosphorus for the root, and potash for the stems, flowers, and fruit, though they are very interrelated. The balance is extremely important. Too high a proportion of nitrogen may make the plant weak and spindly; too much phosphorus may make it tough and keep it from growing well; too much potash will retard growth and cause premature blooming. Remember, it is the balance which is important, not the amounts. The percentages tell you how much of each you are using.

With plants you can't "stuff the goose." Too much fertilizer will cause "burning" or the drying-up of the plant because of the high amounts of these materials, nitrogen and potash, which are "salts," cause water to move out of the plant into the ground (the area of high salt concentration) rather than into the plant as it should. The high salt concentration also damages the feeder roots and prevents water uptake. The effect of too much fertilizer is often mistaken for lack of moisture in the soil since the symptoms are similar.

The proper amount of fertilizer is absolutely necessary to grow a good crop. Too much fertilizer is dangerous; too little prevents proper growth.

In addition, the proper method of fertilizing plants is one of the most important things a gardener must learn. Though I can tell you the general rules, much depends on the particular climatic conditions of a given season. You must learn a lot for yourself through practice and experience.

During high rainfall, the very soluble nutrients, nitrogen and potash, will dissolve in the soil water and be leached outside of the root zone. During dry periods, the fertilizer does not enter the roots of the plant because of the lack of moisture to dissolve it. More fertilizer, or perhaps fertilizer more often, is necessary during seasons with lots of rain since so much is being leached from the root zone of the plant and is never used.

The best way to determine fertilizer needs while the plant is growing is to watch it carefully. Changes from a dark green to a light green or yellow-green color, slow or weak growth, lack of blossoms, poor fruit development, and even the plant's drying up will indicate whether too little or too much fertilizer is being made available to the plant.

Growing Medium Requirement

The growing medium is the last requirement. This is the soil I have talked so much about. The structure is important, especially in our Southern gardens which are so heavy in clay. Take note of your soil conditions and use every piece of advice I have given and every bit of knowledge you can gain to improve your soil. Unless the soil is good, nothing will grow properly.

This has been true throughout the ages, and Jesus used this fact to point out other great truths when he gave the parable of the seed sower.

Good soil, well prepared is absolutely necessary to be a successful vegetable grower.

Plants grown in good soil will flourish and perform well.

Remember how the seed sown on rocky ground sprouted and wilted in the sun, while the seed planted in good soil flourished? These same truths still apply, so treat your soil as if nothing will happen until you enrich the soil.

But good soil alone will not produce a crop. You must work it before you plant and keep it loose and friable throughout the growing season so that moisture and air can enter and toxic gases can escape. Cultivation with a plow, tiller, or hand tool not only removes competing weeds, but also keeps the soil loose.

One of the best growers I have ever known, Johnny Huyck, who was our farm manager in Egypt, used to say that a field needed fertilizing with iron. He didn't mean adding some iron solution to the tops of the plants; he meant cultivating with an iron implement. It was just like fertilizing because it really made the plants grow.

Constant cultivation contributes to better growth because it keeps the soil loose and well-aerated, allowing better root growth and deeper penetration. Cultivating also often prevents the surface of the soil from baking hard, thus allowing better water penetration. And finally, removal of weeds by cultivation eliminates competition for water and fertilizer.

Mulching in the South is another important step toward a good harvest. Heavy mulching not only prevents weeds but also keeps the soil from baking dry. Look under a heavy mulch sometime and you will see the soil still loose and friable and filled with moisture, just as it was when the plants were set and the mulch applied.

Improper Training

Improper training methods can also affect the growth of your plants. Vine plants must have room to grow, either up or out. In the type descriptions, I have tried to explain the different training methods. You must realize their importance and train your plants so that they will reach their full potential.

Insects and Diseases

Finally, insects and diseases seem to be always with us. Sometimes they are hardly noticeable; sometimes they cause dramatic damage. This is why you must watch your garden so carefully. You will see sudden changes in the look of the plants as soon as disease or insect damage occur. A few off-color leaves; sudden holes; sudden poor growth; leaves, flowers, or fruits on the ground—all indicate an outside force at work. You must become a detective and discover the cause.

It is easier to identify insects and diseases if you know what might be happening. The plant descriptions of various vegetables have given the most common problems of each. Start with these and look for the culprit. If you can't find any causal agent, take a leaf, fruit, or other affected part to your County Extension agent, garden store, or some local expert where you will probably find the answer. Once you know the cause, depend on these experts to suggest the proper control. I have noted only a few of these controls because frequent changes occur in the pest control world with EPA regulations varying from month to month. What each of us uses today may be obsolete tomorrow.

THE GARDENER'S FAITH

The growing garden is a small world in which a great deal can happen. The joy of gardening is learning how the elements of growth are working before your very eyes. It is responding to what you see going on and giving your knowledge and wisdom a chance to figure out how to overcome every obstacle before you.

It takes great faith to be a gardener. When you put a tiny tomato or lettuce seed in the soil and have dreams of beautiful, round, firm tomatoes and gorgeous green heads of lettuce several months away, you must have faith—faith in the seed, faith in your gardening ability, and faith in God and the nature He created that all your efforts will lead to a bountiful harvest.

HARVESTING YOUR CROPS

The fruits of your labor in the garden make all the hard work and perhaps most of the disappointment worth it. A large basket of tomatoes, a mess of beans, a sack of corn, and a myriad of other wonderful vegetables pulled fresh and brought to the kitchen is reward enough for the time and effort you've spent. Add to this the joy and excitement of being productive, and you have the best definition of gardening.

There is a tremendous amount of difference between the taste and quality of what you bring in fresh and what you buy in the produce section of the store. The difference is not just in tomatoes and corn, but in beans and carrots and beets and almost all the others.

Pull greens before they flower, or they may be tough.

Unfortunately, much of this superiority in taste and quality can be negated by poor harvesting techniques and post-harvest handling. There is an art to harvesting and post-harvest handling which will greatly improve the lasting quality of your garden-fresh vegetables.

WHEN TO HARVEST

The first concern of every gardener is to pick his vegetables at the optimum time. Of course this varies from crop to crop, but there are some general rules to follow.

Green crops like beans and leafy vegetables are much better when pulled less than mature rather than over-mature. I prefer tiny fine beans to those which show the bulges of the seed. Greens like spinach, chard, turnips, mustard, and rape are best when younger, though it is all right for greens like kale and collards to be more mature.

Corn should be pulled on the immature side because the older it gets, the more starchy the kernels will be. Usually the best time to pull is when the kernels meet between the rows.

Melons are best when on the ripe, rather than the immature side. The greatest amount of sugar is made at the time the melon reaches its peak. See the type description section for pulling suggestions.

Squash, cucumbers, and zucchini should be pulled when less mature; baking or winter squash should be pulled when the skin is hard.

Head lettuce must be harvested when the head first reaches the firm round stage. There is a serious chance that the lettuce will bolt and go to seed if it is left too long in the garden. When you can place your hand on top of the head and still wrap the ends of your fingers around the ball slightly, the head is an ideal size.

Cabbage grown in the spring should be pulled as soon as the head is well-formed. There is always the danger of loopers (green worms) getting into the head in the garden. Fall cabbage may be left to pull as needed until cold weather arrives.

Sweet corn should be pulled as soon as the kernels are meeting on the cob. When the silks first turn brown, the ear should be ready.

Cut cabbage as soon as possible when large enough so that it will not be attacked by worms.

Cut cauliflower as soon as the head is white. Too much sun will cause the "curds" to turn dark.

Broccoli is no good if allowed to bloom before harvesting.

Broccoli and cauliflower are harvested when the heads are full, but neither should be left too long. Broccoli beads will quickly turn yellow (bloom) and cauliflower curds will darken if left too long, especially if the days are sunny and warm.

Harvest root crops like beets, carrots, radishes, and turnips at the size suggested in the vegetable descriptions rather than waiting until they are large; all of them will get pithy and tasteless if left in the ground too long, especially in the early summer. The fall crop may be left longer than the spring crop.

Green onions may be pulled whenever they are of a size suitable for your needs, but leave large onions in the ground to mature. Large onions are mature when the tops break over and start yellowing. The same is true of garlic and shallots.

Irish potatoes are dug when the tops begin to die, and sweet potatoes are dug when the fall's first frost nips the leaves.

For the best quality and taste, tomatoes should be pulled in the full pink or light red stage, which is just before full maturity. The sugar content is made at this time, yet the tomato is still firm and not mushy.

There has been a great change in the eating habits of Southern people. Until recently, it was unheard of for people to eat squash, cauliflower, broccoli, spinach, English peas, and even beans raw. Now these vegetables are widely used in salads and as vehicles for dips. This use is possible only when the vegetable is pulled in a very immature stage.

Root crops, like beets, will become pithy and tough if grown too large before harvesting.

Tomatoes should be deep pink or turning red at harvest time so that they will have the maximum taste.

Harvest green onions while they are still standing straight and while young and tender.

HANDLING AFTER HARVEST

Post-harvest handling is also extremely important. Scientists have done some extraordinary work in this area to increase the shelf life of vegetables tremendously.

The gardener should be aware of the rapid deterioration which can occur with improper handling of fresh vegetables. Heat is one of the real enemies of good quality, but cold is also destructive. Do not store tomatoes below 50 degrees F. until they have reached full maturity. Hold broccoli at 32 to 33 degrees F. almost from the moment of harvest.

The Cold Bath Treatment

The first rule is to harvest quickly and take the vegetables out of the sun and heat of the garden as soon as possible. As I described each vegetable, I made suggestions as to cold bath treatments for many of them. This treatment takes the heat out of the fleshy part of many vegetables like lettuce (especially the head types), broccoli, and cauliflower. This is important because the heart of the lettuce and the stems of broccoli and cauliflower will retain a lot of heat, and the metabolism of the plant will actually increase the heat in that area. I have seen broccoli, which was given the cold bath treatment but packed with too little air movement, actually rot in the cartons due to the intense core heat. Head lettuce from the market has a brown center on occasion. This is caused by poor cooling in the fields; even though the lettuce may have been stored at near

Cold bath treatment of green onions is helpful. The bunch on the bottom was given a cold bath and kept cold while the one on the top was just kept in a cool place without treatment. Philippines.

freezing, the center remained warm enough to begin rotting. The following vegetables should be given the cold bath treatment:

Broccoli	Leek	Shallot (for green tops)
Canteloupe	Lettuce	Spinach
Cauliflower	Spring onion	Swiss chard
Celery	Radish	Turnip greens (and Mustard)
Honeydew		

The cold bath treatment is easy and can become an addition to the regular washing procedure. After thorough washing, fill the sink about halfway with ice cubes and the rest of the way with water. After the water is very cold, plunge the vegetables into the cold bath. Broccoli, cauliflower, celery, leek, spring onions, radish, shallots, and lettuce should remain for 10–15 minutes. Melons should be bathed for 5 to 10 minutes and greens for about 5 minutes. As soon as the vegetables are removed from the bath, refrigerate them immediately.

Remember, the cold bath treatment is good for storage only and is not necessary if the vegetable is going to be eaten immediately. However, any time the vegetable is going into the refrigerator, even if for only a day or two, the cold bath is effective in keeping garden quality.

Washing Vegetables

All vegetables should be washed before eating. This is generally done immediately after harvesting except in the case of potatoes, large onions, garlic, and shallots grown for bulbs which are to be stored.

I want my vegetables free from grit, chemicals, and insects before I eat them, so washing is a ritual in my kitchen.

Storing Vegetables For Later Use

You can store many vegetables for some length of time before they are eaten. Some, like potatoes, onion bulbs, horseradish, Jerusalem artichoke, winter squash, and pumpkins, may last for many months under proper conditions. Others like carrots, beets, radishes, and cabbages will last for many weeks, while many like tomatoes, lettuce, the many greens, melons, and broccoli will last only a week or a few days.

In each vegetable description I have tried to give you some indication of the storage time. Follow the storage recommendations so that you can gain as much shelf time as possible from your crops.

CHAPTER 4

FRUITS FOR THE SOUTH

The culture of fruiting plants has been of great importance throughout history. The Bible is filled with references to the fruits commonly grown in the Holy Land including grapes, the fruits of the vine, and figs which were used in many of Jesus's parables to teach greater meanings by using common everyday experiences.

People of the Mediterranean, Europe, and the Orient practiced the art of fruit culture from the earliest recorded time. They devised many interesting methods of growing fruiting plants in areas which did not have a suitable climate. The art of espalier was developed to allow the heat from walls to ripen fruits brought from warmer and sunnier habitats. During the age of exploration, large numbers of "new" fruits were brought from faraway places to be received as enthusiastically as were the much-sought spices and jewels.

Today, fruit is one of the most important foods of the table. Fruits are a source of a broad number of the vitamins and minerals which should be an important part of our diets. Modern nutritional experts advise us to eat more fruit as a replacement for foods which are high in refined sugar. As we learn more and more about the nutritional value of fruits, we are constantly searching for new and exotic types which will add variety to our diets.

The art of espalier

Supermarkets are now filled with an extraordinary variety of well-known as well as unusual fruits from all over the world to satisfy this growing demand. It is not uncommon to find such exotic items as Kiwi, Starfruit, Mangosteen, Mangoes, Chickoo, Carambola, and Lychees along with the more common and well-known bananas and pineapples. Besides these tropical fruits, the supermarkets feature apples, pears, peaches, plums, cherries, grapes, berries, avocados, and a number of citrus fruits which are produced here in our own country.

One of the great rewards of working in tropical countries has been the discovery of many fruits which I never knew existed. I have eaten Jackfruit, Breadfruit, Chico, Durian, Papaya, Guava, and Rambutan. Some I have liked; some I have not. All are, however, interesting to try. Eating them has given me a much greater appreciation for the tremendous variety which nature so generously supplies.

In the South we are fortunate in having a wide range of temperate-zone fruits which we can grow in our gardens. This is one of the great rewards for living in our part of the world.

A banana plantation in the Philippines

Jackfruit in the Philippines   Pineapple in the Philippines

Rabbiteye Blueberries, one of our most
successful fruits

Mangoes in the Philippines

Durian, a prized fruit of
tropical southeast Asia

Today the vegetable garden has assumed tremendous relevance because of the poor quality of so many fresh vegetables which are shipped from far-off places. Much of the same relevance is applicable to fruits. Home-grown strawberries have a sweetness unknown in the market. Fresh-picked blueberries, apples right off the tree, pears taken directly to the table, and grapes from which you make your own jelly; all are better.

Some fruits, like raspberries, are grown for the economics. These highly-perishable fruits are so costly that having them in the back yard is immensely worthwhile.

Some fruits are grown for the pure enjoyment of harvesting your own. But peaches, plums, and cherries, on the other hand, require a lot of work and having them takes special dedication.

Also, many fruits may be used as ornamentals because their blossoms rival those of flowering trees, and the added bonus of the harvest is exciting. Others, like pecans, make excellent shade trees as well as fruit bearers.

We can approach fruit growing, therefore, as an adjunct to the landscape design or as a whole new facet of gardening.

Here are some criteria which are important to follow since fruits, like all other plants, have special needs:
- Almost all do best in at least six hours of full sun.
- Fruits need good soil and excellent drainage.
- Avoid low areas where frost settles, for you may lose the blossoms of the early-flowering types.
- Fruits need proper pruning and training.
- Disease and insect control is essential in most cases.
- Yearly fertilizing is necessary.

Choose carefully the fruits you wish to grow, considering the special needs of each. Decide ahead of planting whether you are ready to assume the programs needed to produce the quality which will make the effort worthwhile.

Apple blossoms are a great addition to the spring landscape.

The fall color of the blueberry is a beautiful red.

A fruiting plum offers great beauty when it blossoms.

A fruiting pear is as beautiful as most flowering trees.

FRUITS IN THE LANDSCAPE

TYPE	ALTERNATE USE	FEATURE
APPLE	Ornamental flowering tree	Pink spring flowers
BLUEBERRY	Background shrub	Flowers in the spring
CHERRY	Ornamental tree	Pink spring flowers
CHINESE CHESTNUT	Shade tree	Spreading tree
CRABAPPLE	Flowering tree	Pink spring flowers
FIG	Espalier, background shrub	Heavy leaves and limbs
GRAPE	Fence and arbor cover	Heavy leaves, fruits
MUSCADINE	Fence and arbor cover	Heavy foliage, fruits
PEACH	Ornamental flowering tree	Pink spring blossoms
PECAN	Shade tree	Large spreading tree
PEAR	Ornamental flowering tree	Early white blossoms
PLUM	Ornamental flowering tree	Early white or pink blossoms
RASPBERRY	Fence cover	White flowers, fruit
SCUPPERNONG	Fence and arbor cover	Heavy leaves and fruit
STRAWBERRY	In containers or beds	Attractive plant and fruit
WALNUT	Shade tree	Good structure

The flowers of a fruiting peach are most colorful in the spring.

CHOOSING WHICH FRUITS TO GROW

Many types of fruits grow well in the South. That does not mean you will want to grow every fruit which is possible to grow. Two considerations which will bear upon your choices are the time and effort you wish to spend, and whether your orchard site is good enough to grow easily the wide number of types which may interest you. Your County Extension Service will be happy to advise you. Most have excellent bulletins on each fruit recommended for your specific area.

The following chart is based on my general experience, and is taken primarily from my own efforts and those of gardening friends.

NAME	EASE OF GROWING	WORST PROBLEMS
APPLE	Medium	Insects, diseases, pollination
APRICOT	Very hard	Diseases, frost on flowers
BLACKBERRY	Medium	Proper pruning is necessary
BLUEBERRY	Easy	Must have acid soil
BOYSENBERRY	Hard	Proper pruning, heat
CHERRY	Medium	Diseases
CHINESE CHESTNUT	Easy	Pollination
CRABAPPLE	Easy	Diseases and borers
DEWBERRY	Medium	Proper pruning, heat
FIG	Easy except for cold	Cold damage
GRAPE	Medium	Proper pruning, diseases
MUSCADINE	Medium	Proper pruning, fertilizing
NECTARINE	Very hard	Insects and diseases
PEACH	Hard	Insects and diseases
PEAR	Easy	Fire Blight bacterial disease
PECAN	Easy	Getting established
PERSIMMON	Easy except for cold	Cold damage, getting established
PLUM	Hard	Insects and diseases
POMEGRANATE	Easy except for cold	Cold damage
RASPBERRY	Hard	Insects, diseases, heat
STRAWBERRY	Easy	Proper culture

ALLOWING GROWING SPACE

Many fruit trees grow very large; others are smaller-growing. Your available space will determine which types you can grow. Crowding fruit trees will cause poor growth, poor blossoming, and poor harvest. Tall-growing fruits like pecans and walnuts must be planted so that they will not shade smaller-growing fruit trees and vines. Each plant must receive ample sun. Crowding or placing too near taller-growing trees will reduce yields because of shading.

In the landscape, fruit trees are best grown with ample open space around them so that their beauty can be appreciated. The following chart gives the general spacing for both standard and dwarf fruits. Since individual cultivars will vary somewhat, always ask what the spacing should be for a new cultivar. The dwarfs will also vary according to the root stock used as the dwarfing agent. Always ask about the spacing of the particular stock on which the trees are grown.

NAME	STANDARD SPACING	DWARF SPACING	BEARING AGE
APPLE	25 feet	10 to 15 feet	3 to 7 years
APRICOT	20 feet	10 feet	3 years
BLACKBERRY	3 to 6 feet		2 years
BLUEBERRY	4 to 10 feet		2 years
BOYSENBERRY	3 to 5 feet		2 years
CHERRY	20 feet	10 feet	3 years
CHINESE CHESTNUT	35 feet		3 to 4 years
CRABAPPLE	15 to 20 feet		3 years
DEWBERRY	3 to 5 feet		2 years
FIG	12 feet		2 to 3 years
GRAPE	16 feet		2 years
LOGANBERRY	3 to 5 feet		2 years
MUSCADINE	20 feet		2 to 3 years
NECTARINE	25 feet		3 to 4 years
PEACH	25 feet	15 feet	3 to 4 years
PEAR	20 feet	15 feet	3 to 4 years
PECAN	35 to 40 feet		5 to 7 years
PERSIMMON	15 feet		3 to 5 years
PLUM	20 feet	10 feet	3 years
POMEGRANATE	10 feet		2 to 3 years
RASPBERRY	3 to 5 feet		2 years
STRAWBERRY	18 × 24 inches		1 year
WALNUT, ENGLISH	35 feet		5 to 6 years

DEVELOPING A HOME ORCHARD

Many gardeners use fruits in the landscape, which is a perfectly feasible alternative when space is limited. When there is room, however, it is best to develop a home orchard just as you develop a vegetable or flower garden.

CHOOSING THE SITE

Fruits, as I have said, need as much sun as possible with a minimum of six full hours. Choose open ground as far from other trees as possible to eliminate root competition.

Fruits need well-drained, high-quality soil. They do poorly if the soil is heavy clay and stays sticky and wet.

Air circulation is important. Choose high ground if possible because low areas are prone to late frosts and because muggy evening air in the summer encourages the development of diseases.

LAYING OUT YOUR ORCHARD

Plan your orchard carefully. Each type of fruit will need to be together for cross-pollination and ease of spraying, pruning, and fertilizing.

Determine where you will plant the bush fruits, like raspberries, because they will need a two or three-wire fence on which the canes will be trained. Likewise, place grapes and muscadines so that they are easily fenced. Run the rows of grapes and muscadines north and south, or as near as possible to that so that sun will fall evenly on both sides of the row.

PLANTING THE ORCHARD

Plant fruits when they are dormant, or from the first killing frost in the fall until blossoming time in the spring. I much prefer fall and early winter planting because the new roots will begin to develop before the leaves put out, and as a result the first year's growth will be stronger.

Fruits may be purchased in a number of different ways. They may be balled, either machine balled or balled and burlapped, in a container, or bare root. Generally, older trees are balled or container grown while younger trees may be satisfactorily grown from bare root, packaged plants.

I prefer planting the younger one-year or two-year trees because they are easier to start training through proper pruning, and they are generally easier to get to live. Also, when properly planted, a young tree will begin growth faster and will catch up and perhaps even pass a larger, more expensive tree within a year or two.

Vine crops like grapes and muscadines are usually bare rooted and sold in packages. I prefer a two-year plant especially in the case of muscadines which have a relatively poor root system when only one year old.

Strawberries are usually sold in packages and are one-year daughter plants. These are ideal for home garden settings.

Orchard plantings are accomplished by digging holes for each individual tree or plant because planting distances are too far apart for most of

Dig a hole larger and deeper than the root system.

Mix ground bark or peat moss, perlite (if soil drains poorly), and soil from the hole until the mixture is loose and friable.

Place the roots in the hole at a depth so that the graft union is above the surface of the soil.

Place the prepared soil mixture around the roots.

Pack the soil tightly to prevent air pockets in the soil. Be sure the graft union is above the surface of the surrounding soil. DO NOT PLANT TOO DEEPLY.

Make a collar around the outer edge of the hole which you dug. Water thoroughly to settle the soil around the roots and to start new root development.

us to work the entire area. Great care must be taken to dig the hole much larger than the root system of the plant and to properly prepare the soil which is to be placed around the roots in the hole.

Dig the hole wider and deeper than the root system of the plant. If the soil is poorly drained, dig the hole even deeper and put at least four inches of bark chunks or coarse gravel in the bottom. Prepare the soil for packing around the roots by adding one-third ground bark and one-third peat moss to one-third soil which was removed from the hole. Mix this thoroughly.

Plant carefully, never deeper than the trees were growing in the nursery. This is most important. Also, pack the soil tightly around the roots. Water thoroughly to drive out any air pockets which may have been left around the roots.

PRUNING AND TRAINING

The art of pruning fruiting plants is ancient. There are many Biblical references to the pruning of the vine (grape) and the fig for it was known, even in those ancient days, that good fruit only occurred after proper pruning.

The principle is rather simple. Prune to force the growth on which the bloom buds will form for the next year's fruit, and prune to thin the number of flower buds so that the number of fruits which are set during the current year can be properly sustained by the tree.

Very few fruits will produce well without proper pruning and training. For instance, peaches will grow, if left natural, in an upright oval shape which allows only a minimal amount of fruit to develop on the outer shell. We must alter the natural shape of a peach tree by pruning to open it up and allow more room for the shoots to develop and set flowering buds. Opening up the top also gives better air movement, fewer disease problems, and more chance for sun to ripen the fruit. This is called the **Open Head** or **Basket** method of pruning.

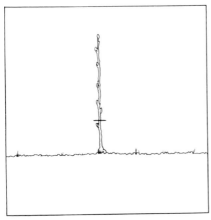

First year pruning for the open head method of pruning. Cut the single stem back to 18 or 24 inches to form a low, upward growing tree.

If you purchase a two-year-old tree it must be cut back severely or the tree will always be top-heavy and a poor producer.

Second year pruning for the open head method. Choose three to four heavy, upward growing branches to form the structure of the tree. Remove all others. Cut back the remaining branches to an outside bud.

Always prune just above outward-facing bud. Prune out inside growth to encourage an open center.

First year pruning for the modified leader method. Remove the terminal (top) bud. Should there be any side branches, choose the strongest and remove the terminal buds on each remaining branch.

Second year pruning for the modified leader method. Remove the terminal bud. Remove any branches which have a narrow angle with the trunk. Cut back the remaining side branches to an outside bud.

REMOVE VERTICAL WATER SPROUTS

Water sprouts are very rapid-growing (24 to 36 inches in one season) and take strength away from the good, productive growth (which may grow 6 to 12 inches per season). Remove them.

The principle of making an open head is to cut the main trunk back to eighteen to twenty-four inches and to encourage three or four scaffold branches to grow outward from around this area. This leaves an open area in the center of the developing tree. This method of pruning is used on the shorter-lived trees such as peaches and plums as well as those fruits which are most susceptible to rot diseases.

The second major pruning system for fruit trees is the **Oval** or **Modified Leader** method. The principle of this system is to preserve the natural shape of the tree but to strengthen it so that it will be able to support the heavy weight of the fruit on the outer branches where they form.

This is done by removing the tip or terminal growth bud of the main trunk each year for three or four years to slow down its upward growth while increasing the diameter of the trunk. At the same time, limbs are chosen which have a wide angle with the trunk. These limbs are also tipped to slow their growth and increase their diameter in relation to their length. Limbs of these trees should also be spaced at least eighteen inches apart.

Bush berries only produce fruit on second-year wood. Once a cane has borne, it should be removed. It will never bear again, and if not removed will leave the bramble of dead, thorny stalks so common in wild blackberry patches.

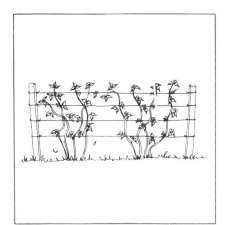

Train bush berries on a fence you can construct in the orchard. Set the posts twelve feet apart and plant two plants between them. Run three or four wires down the line of posts and tie the second-year canes to the wire to help the bush bear the fruit.

Allow the current season's cane growth to arch toward the ground and remain separate from the fruit-bearing cane. The idea is always to keep the new growth separate from the bearing canes. Immediately after harvest, the bearing canes may be removed, and the current season's growth is then tied to the fence.

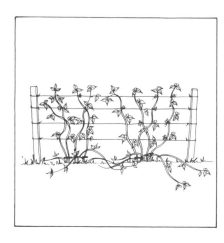

Fruiting wood of a peach

Fruiting spur of a pear

Fruiting spur of an apple

Fruiting spur of a plum

The Modified Leader system is used on types of fruits which are long-lived and set their fruit on the outer part of the limbs. Pears and apples fall into this category.

The special pruning techniques for grapes, bush berries, and figs are discussed under each of these groups.

I have received hundreds of calls about fruits not bearing properly. Investigation of these individual problems often reveals a lack of understanding of what part of the plant sets the flower and thus the fruit. This is particularly true of apples, pears, and plums which set their buds on "trashy"-looking wood called fruiting spurs. Very often the new orchardist mistakes these spurs for poor growth and removes it. The result is little or no fruit. Watch your fruiting plants when they blossom and identify the wood on which the blossom forms. Carefully leave this wood when doing your pruning.

We see that each type of fruit takes its own special pruning method. This training starts when you first set out the plant and continues through the life of the plant. It is one of the most important aspects of good fruit production and should be done each winter while the plants are thoroughly dormant. December and January are ideal times to prune fruits. Put it on your gardening calendar and do it every year without fail.

SUCKERING

One of the more confounding occurrences in growing many fruits is, after several years of normal production, the sudden emergence of an inferior fruit on part or all of the plant. This "reversion" is baffling to most home owners and often leads to speculation that their tree has "gone bad."

The explanation for this problem is relatively simple and may be easily prevented with a basic understanding of how many fruits are propagated.

Apples, apricots, cherries, nectarines, peaches, pears, pecans, and plums are grafted trees. This means that the cultivar is budded or grafted on a vigorous understock which is genetically different. This procedure provides the tree with a stronger and more vigorous root system which may be more pest-resistant than the roots of the cultivar. There are a tremendous number of advantages in this system. However, there is also a potential problem of which the home orchardist must be aware.

The understock may, at any time during the life of the tree, sprout growth which is referred to as suckers. These shoots, which come from beneath the graft or bud union, will have the characteristics of the root stock rather than the cultivar itself. Since the understock is different, the fruit will also be different and almost always useless.

Watch carefully for this growth from beneath the graft or bud union and remove it immediately. Do not allow it to develop into an alternative tree which will overcome your cultivar. Removal should be done when the suckers are young and tender. It is best to pull these off rather than to remove them by cutting. This pulls the sprouting bud off and helps to prevent resprouting which often occurs when cutting and leaving some of the wood of the sucker.

Fruits which are grown from cuttings, like grapes, muscadines, and blueberries; those grown from divisions, like blackberries, dewberries, and raspberries; those grown from daughter plants, like strawberries; and those grown from seeds, like Chinese chestnuts and walnuts, do not have this type of suckering problem though basal shoots should never be allowed to develop a competitive growth to your plant.

Suckers from the roots of an apple. This tree is over 35 years old and still suckers.

Note the short internodes which indicates the very slow growth rate resulting in dwarfness.

Genetically dwarf Mandarin Peach

DWARF FRUITS

Dwarf fruit trees have special appeal for the home orchardist. More trees may be planted in a given area than with standard size fruit trees.

There are two types of dwarf trees: fruits which are genetically or naturally dwarf like *North Star* cherry and *Mandarin* peach, and fruits which are artificially dwarfed like apples, pears, and peaches.

Artificial dwarfing is done by grafting the cultivar upon a root stock which is smaller and more restricted than that of the cultivar itself.

When using artificially dwarfed trees be diligent about suckers which come readily from the dwarfing stock, especially when an interstem graft is used. This procedure produces the semi-dwarf apple trees by placing a piece of the dwarfing agent between the common understock and the cultivar.

It is wise to stake artificially dwarfed trees since the weight of the fruit and the heavy top growth of the cultivar, along with the smaller root system, may cause blow-down during heavy rain and wind storms.

INSECT AND DISEASE CONTROL

A spray program is essential for good, high-quality fruit. The orchardist must be aware that there are three facets to insect and disease control on fruits. The first is to protect the tree from damage by bark and wood insects and the second is to protect the foliage from insects and diseases. The third is to protect the fruit from insects and diseases. Timing is most

A complete spray program is required to overcome problems like this brown rot on a plum.

Be prepared to spray if you are going to grow many of our Southern fruits.

important in controlling all of these problems and the first spraying, unfortunately, occurs when few of us have it on our minds. This is the dormant or winter spray which is very effective against a number of diseases and some insects.

I will discuss these programs in a general way under each fruit listing. Your County Extension Service will have available specific recommendations for control measures and times of application for your area. Before you go too far with your home orchard, be sure and ask for one of these spray guides.

The spray season starts with dormant sprays in the winter. The next spraying is at blossom time, and then spraying continues on a regular basis until right before harvest. Not all fruits require this much spraying, but for those types which do, it is a must.

SELECTING CULTIVARS

Choosing the right cultivar of fruit often means the difference between success and failure. Fruit cultivars are very specific as to the regions in which they will perform well, and you must take special care to choose the best ones for the South.

You may have to sacrifice some excellent qualities which you like in exchange for cultivars which will grow in this region. For instance, most of the high-quality pears which you receive in a gift box have absolutely superb taste and texture, but these cultivars are highly susceptible to Fire Blight. Fire Blight is so devastating in the South that a Bartlett pear planted here will live only a few years, and perhaps may never even reach fruiting age. The huge delicious Smyrna figs will not grow here, and so we must depend on Southern figs for our plantings. Always question your fruit tree dealer or pay special attention to what the catalogue says to be sure your new plant is suitable for the South. Your County Extension Service bulletins are a good place to start. They will list the proven cultivars, but they may not list the newest introductions, which may be perfectly superb and have decided advantages over the older listed cultivars.

There are other considerations when choosing cultivars. I always recommend starting with the earliest-ripening cultivars of those types which need a lot of spraying. Early plums are better for the home orchard than later ones because you do not have to spray as much. Remember: A plum ripening in mid-June will take three or four fewer sprayings than one ripening in mid-July, and the late May and June weather is much less conducive to disease development than late June and July.

Many types of fruits must have a given number of cold hours to cause good flowering and fruit formation. Gardeners living in the southern part of the region must pay particular attention to the number of cold hours each cultivar must have in order to choose the ones most likely to fruit satisfactorily.

Many fruits may be self-sterile; that is, pollen from one cultivar will not be viable on the same plant. *Orient* pears, some plums, and many apples are self-sterile and must have other cultivars nearby to provide the viable pollen to set their fruit. In the case of Chinese chestnuts or peaches, one tree will cross-pollinate another, whereas pollen from a given tree will not satisfactorily pollinate itself. When choosing cultivars, always find out if the cultivar is self-sterile so that you can add pollinators to the plantings if necessary.

Muscadines are either female, male, or in some cases, bisexual. A male or bisexual vine must be added for pollination if the cultivar has only female flowers. The old favorite cultivar, *Scuppernong*, is among the female types and should always have a source of pollen from another cultivar. Bunch grapes, like *Concord* and *Fredonia*, are self-fertile.

The Southland Muscadine is a bisexual cultivar.

ALL ABOUT FRUITS FOR THE SOUTH

APPLE
Malus sylvestris

Method of pruning: Modified Leader
Pollination problems: Most are self-unfertile
Ornamental value: Excellent
Best cultivars: 'Anna' - red cheek - late June; 'Lodi' - yellow - July; 'Jerseymac' - red - July; 'Red Delicious' - red - late August; 'Golden Delicious' - yellow - early September; 'Red Stayman' - red - October; 'Granny Smith' - green - late October; 'Yates' - small red - late October

The apple is a home orchard favorite for its ease in growing and its ornamental value. It is a long-lasting fruit tree, for most of us, almost infinite. I had an old apple tree in my yard which was pushing 100 years when a storm finally blew it down.

Plant apples as one-year whips or two-year branched trees. I prefer the former because it is easier to start the branching then. Use the Modified Leader method of pruning to strengthen the branches, which will have to hold enormous weights of fruits. Continue pruning each year to remove weak wood, water sprouts, and cross branches, and to maintain the strength of the branches.

Choose the cultivars carefully so that cross-pollination and flower fertilization are assured. Few cultivars will set fruit from their own pollen, so the wise gardener plants more than one cultivar. Check the catalogue listings carefully or obtain County Extension bulletins which give the cross-pollination indexes for each cultivar.

Fertilize each year with about one-half pound of a 10-10-10 formula per year of age of the tree up to a maximum of 15 pounds per tree. In later years, when the trees are structurally secure, you can substitute ammonium nitrate, but cut down the amount to a maximum of five pounds.

Since insects and diseases will attack apples, you should keep to a regular spray program. For details in your area, obtain an apple spray guide from your nursery or Extension Service.

Dwarf forms are available for many cultivars. In most of the South, the semi-dwarfs are better than the dwarfs, and they are highly recommended for use in the home orchard.

APRICOT
Prunus Armeniaca

Method of pruning: Open head
Pollination problems: Plant at least two
Ornamental value: Good, except blossom loss from frost is common
Best cultivars: 'Early Golden,' 'Goldcot'

Yellow Delicious Apple

Red Stayman Winesap Apple

Lodi Apple

Apples are pruned using the Modified Leader method.

Since we do not live in apricot country, only the daring should try to grow them. Our late frosts almost always kill the flowers, and diseases are worse than on the peaches.

BLACKBERRY
Rubus sp.

Method of pruning: Keep only one and two-year growth
Pollination problems: None
Ornamental value: May be used on fences
Best cultivars: 'Thornless' or others locally recommended; I particularly like the cultivar 'Flint'

Cultivated blackberries are much larger and better than the roadside ones we have so much fun picking on a Sunday afternoon. There are now excellent thornless cultivars which makes growing them much easier.

Blackberries, raspberries, boysenberries, dewberries, and loganberries belong to a group of plants with the unique habit of producing only on second-year wood. Once a cane has borne, it should be removed. It will never bear again, and soon dies to leave the bramble of dead, thorny stalks so common in wild blackberry patches.

Train them on a fence or a berry fence which you can construct in the orchard. Set the posts twelve feet apart and plant two plants between them. Run three or four wires down the line of posts, to which you can tie the canes grown the previous season which will bear the fruit. The current season's cane growth is kept separate by allowing it to arch toward the ground, or I have seen them held away from the fence with long hoops. The idea is always to keep the new growth separate from the bearing canes. Immediately after harvest, the bearing canes may be removed, at which time the current season's growth is tied to the fence.

Blackberries may be attacked by a number of insects and diseases which you can control with a good spray program. Check your latest County Extension bulletins for recommended control measures.

RABBIT-EYE BLUEBERRY
Vaccinium Ashei

Method of pruning: Little is needed except to rejuvenate overgrown or heavily-trunked plants
Pollination problems: Must have two different cultivars
Ornamental value: Excellent as a deciduous flowering shrub
Best cultivars: 'Climax' and 'Woodward,' early-season; 'Briteblue' and 'Tifblue,' mid-season; 'Delite' and 'Baldwin,' late-season

The Southern or Rabbit-eye blueberry is the only one which should be attempted in most of the South. The Highbush types, commonly grown farther north, do not like our soils and climate.

There are many excellent cultivated blackberries which may be grown in the South.

Blackberries are best trained on a wire fence to help segregate one- and two-year growth.

Montmorency Cherry

Tifblue Blueberry

Blueberries require very little pruning or shaping.

The Rabbit-eye blueberries have been greatly improved by selection and breeding at the Georgia Coastal Plains Experiment Station at Tifton. The results are perfectly fantastic blueberries for our Southern gardens.

This fruit is one of the easiest to grow and one of the heaviest producers. It takes little except acidic soil with a pH between 4.0 and 5.2, which is also well-drained and high in humus.

Fertilize sparingly and only with an acidic fertilizer. Never use lime near or on blueberries.

There are few pests except a rare infestation of fruit worms, which should be controlled. Consult your local nurseryman or County Extension Service for the recommended spray.

BOYSENBERRY
Rubus ursinus var. *loganobaccus* cv. '*Boysenberry*'

Method of pruning: Keep only one and two-year growth
Pollination problems: None
Ornamental value: Only as a fence cover
Best cultivars: 'Thornless'

The Boysenberry is an improved Loganberry and affords the gardener a much juicer, larger-lobed fruit than the blackberry. The method of growing is similar to the blackberry except that the new canes tend to run along the ground and must be tied up after the fruiting canes have finished.

CHERRY
Prunus avium, Sweet
Prunus Cerasus, Sour

Method of pruning: Modified Leader
Pollination problems: Plant two different cultivars for best results
Ornamental value: Excellent flowering trees
Best cultivars: In the South, sweet cherries are difficult; the sour red cherries 'Montmorency' and 'North Star' (both small-growing) are most recommended

We are not in sweet cherry country and we should restrict our cherry tree growing to the red or sour type. I have a *North Star* and so does a neighbor. They are excellent and don't grow so large, really being more of a large shrub than a tree. The fruit is also rather sweet and easily edible when picked fresh off the tree.

I have never had much problem with *North Star*, though all cherries are supposed to be sprayed on a regular schedule.

CHINESE CHESTNUT
Castanea mollissima

Method of pruning: Only to remove poor growth
Pollination problems: Must have plantings of at least two, but preferably three

Ornamental value: Beautiful low-spreading tree
Best cultivars: Most are grown from seed and no named cultivars are needed

The Chinese chestnut is the modern replacement for the great American chestnut which was destroyed in this country by the Chestnut Blight. The Chinese chestnut is a heavy bearer of excellent-quality nuts.

As soon as the nut comes out of the burr, it should be skinned and boiled, and then frozen for later use. If left for long without boiling, it becomes extremely hard.

The Chinese chestnut has practically no problems except that the burrs on the ground are tough on little boys' bare feet, and on their fathers, who have to remove the stickers carefully, one by one, while the boys scream and wiggle.

CRABAPPLE
Malus sp.

Method of pruning: Modified Leader
Pollination problems: None
Ornamental value: Excellent
Best cultivars: 'Callaway,' 'Dolgo,' and 'Hyslop'

Crabapples are usually considered flowering trees rather than primarily fruit trees. However, the cultivars listed above will produce huge quantities of excellent crabapples for jellies and whatever else one does with crabapples.

Their problems are few, even fewer than those of apples. Pruning is done for strength but is not as exacting as with apples since the fruit has so little weight.

DEWBERRY
Rubus sp.

Method of pruning: Keep only one and two-year growth
Pollination problems: None
Ornamental value: Only as a fence cover
Best cultivars: 'Lucretia'

The dewberry is much like the blackberry except that the canes are more procumbent and are perhaps easier to work with on a fence. Since they tend to run on the ground, a fence is necessary. Pruning and training are the same as for blackberries.

FIG
Ficus carica

Method of pruning: Only to remove dead wood or spindly shoots at the base; heading back may be helpful in harvesting
Pollination problems: None on southern cultivars

Figs are allowed to grow into heavy bushes.

Chinese Chestnut

Crabapple Tree

Grapes are pruned each year by cutting back old wood to two buds.

These grapes are trained on a one-wire fence with an arm going in each direction from the main stem.

Fredonia Grape

Maturing grapes may be bagged to prevent bird damage.

Nets may also be used to prevent bird damage.

Ornamental value: Excellent espalier and background shrub
Best cultivars: 'Magnolia,' 'Brown Turkey' (hardiest), and 'Celeste'

Figs are favorite plants in the South despite the severe damage that has occurred during these terrible below-zero winters. Despite the cold damage every now and then, figs should not be omitted from the orchard, though care should be taken to protect them from cold northwest winds.

They usually do best when planted with a tree line, with other large shrubs, or with a structure on their western side. They like plenty of moisture but should not be in poorly-drained soil.

Plant figs later than other fruits, usually early March, since the young canes are more tender than older ones. They respond to liming and are best fertilized with a 5-10-15 formula applied as the buds begin to swell. Too much nitrogen may prevent the figs from developing well.

In areas where the temperature drops below 10 degrees, protect the stems by mulching heavily with leaf mold or pine straw. Remove any cold damage to the upper canes; the new shoots will still develop fruit.

GRAPE
Vitis Labrusca and Hybrids

Method of pruning: Two- or Four-arm
Pollination problems: None
Ornamental value: Excellent fence or arbor cover
Best cultivars: 'Fredonia,' 'Concord,' 'Niagara'

The American bunch grape type is our best of the table or wine grapes, though recently some of the new French hybrids are proving successful. For the home gardener, the American types are the ones to use.

Grape culture is specific especially as to pruning and training. The plants should be given plenty of space, usually being planted between two posts which are set 14 to 16 feet apart. At the top of the post is strung a heavy wire to support the arms grown from the top of the plant. If the Four-arm method is used, another wire is strung two feet below the top one.

The first-year plant is tied to the top wire, and an arm is trained in each direction along the wire or wires. After the second growing season, each shoot grown the previous season is cut to two side buds. The shoots from these buds produce the blossoms and fruit. Each year thereafter, the shoots from the previous season are cut back to two buds which will make the wood that forms the blossoms and fruit.

Prune when the plants are thoroughly dormant, usually in December or early January. Pruning too late will cause severe "bleeding" and loss of vigor for the plant.

Grapes are subject to Brown Rot and are particularly inviting to Japanese beetles. Develop a spray program to control these attacks.

The ripening grapes are very attractive to birds. Netting the plants or bagging the clusters in plastic bags will prevent the crop from being ruined.

✿ LOGANBERRY
❧ *Rubus ursinus loganobaccus* cv. *'Loganberry'*

Method of pruning: Keep only one and two-year growth
Pollination problems: None
Ornamental value: Only as a fence cover
Best cultivars: The cultivar itself

The Loganberry is very similar to Boysenberry, which is also a cultivar of *Rubus ursinus loganobaccus*. The culture and training is the same as for the Boysenberry.

Both have berries superior to the blackberry, juicier and with larger lobes.

✿ MUSCADINE
❧ *Vitis rotundifolia*

Method of pruning: Two-arm or Double Curtain
Pollination problems: Many are female only; a few are bisexual
Ornamental value: Excellent on fences or arbors
Best cultivars: Female Cultivars: Bisexual Cultivars:
                'Higgins'—bronze   'Magoon'—black
                'Hunt'—black   'Southland'—black
                'Fry'—bronze   'Dixie Red'—red
                'Summit'—bronze   'Cowart'—black
                'Scuppernong'—bronze   'Triumph'—bronze

The muscadine is uniquely Southern, one of the best of all grapes for us. It is easier to grow and less prone to problems than the American grapes or the French hybrids. The old-fashioned *Scuppernong* is a muscadine with a difference, having a unique taste. It should not be confused with bronze muscadine cultivars.

The essential training of the muscadine is the same as described for the American grape, except that the muscadine is more vigorous and should be set between posts which are 20 feet apart. Seldom is the Two-wire method of pruning used, but the Double Curtain can be used instead. Pruning to two buds is also done.

Do not overfertilize muscadines, but they need some 10-10-10 each year. Bearing vines need two applications per year. The first, about two pounds, should be made in March and the second, one pound, in May.

Little spraying is needed because few insects or diseases bother these plants. If Japanese beetles or other insects or diseases attack, get the latest recommendations from your local nursery or County Extension Service.

✿ NECTARINE
❧ *Prunus Persica* var. *nucipersica*

Method of pruning: Open Head or Basket
Pollination problems: It is advisable to have two trees

Old-fashioned Scuppernong arbor

Hunt Muscadine

Muscadines and Scuppernongs are also grown on a one-wire fence but the posts are set 20 feet apart.

Open Head or Basket training on a peach

Hale Haven Peach

Be sure to keep a good cover spray of an insecticide and a fungicide on peaches from this size until ripening.

Heavy, yearly pruning is needed to produce good peaches.

Borers often attack peaches and should be controlled with a special insecticide.

Dixired Peach

Ornamental value: Good spring blossoms
Best cultivars: 'Armking' - early; 'Lexington' - mid-season; 'Red Gold' - late

Nectarines, or fuzzless peaches, will grow where peaches grow and are handled in the same way with the same pruning pattern, spray schedule, and fertilizing practices as peaches.

PEACH
Prunus Persica

Method of pruning: Open Head or Basket
Pollination problems: Planting at least two trees is best
Ornamental value: Good spring flowers
Best cultivars: Many cultivars are suitable; I recommend the early June peaches such as 'Dixired' for the home garden in the South

In the South we are living in peach country. Georgia has been known as the Peach State, though South Carolina produces more. Throughout our region this type of fruit does well.

Unfortunately, peaches (and nectarines) are subject to a large number of insects and diseases. Do not plant any of the fruits unless you are willing to spend the time and effort for a satisfactory spray program starting in the middle of the winter with a dormant spray and continuing through the pre-bloom, bloom, fruit-forming, and ripening stages. Otherwise the production of a good-quality fruit will elude you.

In most of the South, except the Coastal Plain, there is enough cold weather each year to provide the number of chilling hours to break the rest period. In the lower South, use the peach varieties which have very low chilling requirements.

Yearly pruning is essential for good fruit production. Unpruned trees will set more fruits than the tree can mature into sizable, high-quality peaches. Reduce the previous season's growth by removing most of the inside growth (within the center of the tree) and by cutting back last year's growth. You should reduce the fruiting wood by a total of at least fifty per cent. February is the best month to prune throughout most of the South.

Fertilize and lime peaches each year. Most of our soils are too acid for good growth. Peaches need a pH of 6.5 to thrive. In March apply one-half pound of 10-10-10 fertilizer per year of the tree's age up to a maximum of five pounds. In August apply a pound of calcium nitrate per year of the tree's age up to a maximum of four pounds. Use a soil test to determine the amount of lime needed to keep the pH at 6.5.

Insects and diseases are rampant on the fruit and should be controlled with a regular spray program as recommended. The main problem, borers, affect the tree itself and not the fruit. The control of borers occurs at specific times each year. This time is determined by the weather in your locale, and you should consult your local nurseryman or Extension Service for the best time to spray.

❦ PEAR
❧ *Pyrus communis*

Method of pruning: Modified Leader
Pollination problems: Many pears are self-sterile and must have another cultivar to pollinate the flowers and form the fruit; always plant two different cultivars
Ornamental value: Excellent as a small shade tree or spring-flowering tree
Best cultivars: 'Orient' - excellent eating pear; 'Moonglow' - excellent eating pear; 'Starking Delicious' - excellent eating pear (All these are Fire Blight-resistant)

Pears are easy to grow provided you give them well-drained soil, plenty of sun, and since they blossom early, a site where late frosts do not settle. The most devastating problem is Fire Blight and *no* cultivar should be planted in the South unless it is resistant to this disease. Pears are subject to a number of other problems but none are as severe on pears as they are on apples. Regular spray programs are helpful, but spot-spraying when a problem is discovered will usually be enough to allow for a good harvest.

If you don't harvest pears before the fruits mature, the flesh will become gritty and the quality lower. Pull the fruit when the small dots are beginning to look corky and brown, while the skin between the dots is still light green. Store them in a naturally cool place wrapped in newspaper and eat when the skin turns golden and the fruit softens.

❦ PECAN
❧ *Carya illinoinensis*

Method of pruning: Light tip pruning
Pollination problems: Always plant more than one; choose cultivars whose time of male and female blossoms matches
Ornamental value: Excellent shade tree
Best cultivars: 'Stuart,' 'Desirable,' 'Cape Fear'

Pecans are grown as a dual-purpose tree for shade and nuts on most home properties. They grow so large that most of us can ill afford the space needed to grow them as an orchard or grove plant. Thus the practical way to have pecan trees is to grow them as lawn shade trees.

Pecans are difficult to get established because the very long root may reach 30 to 36 inches, which makes hole-digging almost like well-digging. But it must be done right; most plantings done with a post hole digger end up with a high rate of loss. Dig the hole at least 24 inches wide and deep enough to accommodate the long tap root. The soil level must be at the same level as the tree was grown in the nursery. Do not be fooled by the crook, which indicates that this pecan was bud-grafted, which is done higher on the seedling pecan than it is on a peach tree or a rose plant. Many gardeners will plant up to the bud union, which in the case of pecans is much too deep.

Pecans may be slow to sprout but don't despair. I have seen them take until mid-summer to send out the first new leaves. Do not fertilize the soil which is

Moonglow Pear

An Orient Pear has very awkward growth and is difficult to prune using the normal Modified Leader method, but do your best.

Removal of all infected limbs is the best control.

Orient Pear

Fire Blight on pears is a very destructive bacterial disease which first kills the leaves.

Desirable Pecan showing the medium shell.   Cape Fear Pecan has a thinner shell.

Methley Plum is excellent for the South.   Brown Rot is very bad on plums. Trees should be sprayed on a regular basis to prevent this damage.

The Open Head or Basket system of pruning is used on plums.

packed around the roots. Put one-half pound of 10-10-10 fertilizer around the plant a month after planting. Fertilize later in the life of the tree with a special pecan fertilizer to which has been added a proper amount of zinc. Follow the application recommendations of the pecan fertilizer which you buy. The correct time to fertilize is in February of each year.

Pecans have other problems besides the squirrels getting the nuts before you do. Case borers and Scab will affect the quality of the nuts. However, these trees are usually too large to spray by hand, and commercial spraying is expensive. When these pests attack, remember that you have a beautiful shade tree whether you have nuts or not.

PERSIMMON, JAPANESE
Diospyros Kaki

Method of pruning: Limb-tipping to strengthen the branches
Pollination problems: None with 'Tanenashi'
Ornamental value: Attractive small tree, especially when the fruits are ripening after the leaves have fallen
Best cultivar: 'Tanenashi'

The giant Japanese or Oriental persimmon is a wonderful home orchard plant with few problems other than occasional wood loss during extremely cold winters.

'Tanenashi' is an excellent cultivar and the one to use, especially if you are planting only one tree, since it is self-fertile.

The biggest problem with persimmons is getting them established. The root systems are awful. Dig a deep, wide hole to accommodate the roots and keep well-watered when the May drought arrives. Good luck and good eating.

PLUM
Prunus sp.

Method of pruning: Open Head or Basket
Pollination problems: Most, except 'Methley,' need cross-pollination
Ornamental value: Good spring-flowering tree
Best cultivars: 'Methley' - purple skin, red flesh; 'Robusto' - red skin, red flesh; 'Ozark Premier' - red and yellow skin, yellow flesh; 'Explorer' - large fruit, purple skin, amber flesh

Though plums are a wonderful fruit, do not attempt growing them unless you plan to keep a strict spray schedule because they are attacked by a huge number of insects and diseases, especially fruit worms and Brown Rot.

Plant plums where they are not likely to have a late frost settle. Since plum trees blossom very early, a major threat is frost killing the flowers.

Planting, pruning, and fertilizing are similar to the peach.

POMEGRANATE
Punica Granatum

Method of pruning: Very little is needed
Pollination problems: None
Ornamental value: Excellent flowering shrub
Best cultivar: 'Wonderful'

Pomegranates are plants of arid places but may be grown in the lower South in deep, friable soil. During ripening time they need ample moisture to insure good fruit development.

They may be tried in the upper South but may have cold damage if the temperature falls much below 10 degrees.

Pick the fruit while slightly immature to prevent splitting and let them ripen slowly on a warm shelf.

RASPBERRY
Rubus sp.

Method of pruning: Keep only one and two-year growth
Pollination problems: None
Ornamental value: Only as a fence cover
Best cultivars: 'Southland' - red; 'Sunrise' - red; 'Bristol' - black; 'Sodus' - purple

Raspberries are worth the effort if for no reason other than they are delicious and so expensive in the market. Most are not really happy in our heat, but you can have moderately good results with these listed cultivars. The dark ones grow better than the red ones, but who wants a dark raspberry, anyway?

Betsy loves raspberries and I have had 'Sunrise' growing fairly well for a number of years. My major problem is with red spider mites, which must be tended to immediately when they are discovered. I have had excellent control of these mites with Kelthane.

The culture and pruning is the same as for blackberries.

STRAWBERRY
Fragaria X Ananassa

Best cultivars: 'Sunrise' - early; 'Earligo' - early; ' Cardinal' - mid-season; 'Pocahontas' - mid-season; 'Delite' - late; 'Superfection' - everbearing

A strawberry bed is a most prized part of the garden. From a well-planned, well-established bed can be harvested the most delicious berries you will eat, far better, in my opinion, than the huge tasteless monstrosities you get in the market. Home-grown strawberries are fabulous.

There are many methods of growing strawberries. The Matted Row method is the one most often used by home gardeners because you have to do very little runner-pinching, which eliminates much work. I use the Modified Matted Row system. This entails pinching out all daughter plants past the first.

Strawberries at Callaway Gardens

Pocahontas Strawberry

A maturing crop of Carpathian English Walnuts

A large Carpathian English Walnut in Atlanta

I plant strawberries in wide raised beds (ridges) with two rows to the bed and with the plants set a foot apart in each row. Plant two beds side by side with a middle wide enough to till. This allows plenty of room for one daughter plant to develop. Your County Extension Service will tell you the best method for your area.

How many plants should you have? One hundred-fifty plants is usually enough to have 50 early, 50 mid-season, and 50 late-bearing cultivars. Add another 50 if you wish to include some everbearing. This produces plenty of berries for a family of four and a lot to freeze for later use.

ENGLISH or PERSIAN WALNUT
Juglans regia

Method of Pruning: None
Pollination problems: Plant at least two trees
Ornamental value: Excellent shade trees
Best cultivars: 'Carpathian' strain seedlings or 'Colby' or 'Lake'

The 'Carpathian' strain of Persian walnut is hardy enough to stand the winters here in the South.

Plant Persian walnuts in deep, rich, loamy soil for best results and give them plenty of room to grow or at least 40 feet in every direction. They will provide a beautiful shade tree and excellent nuts.

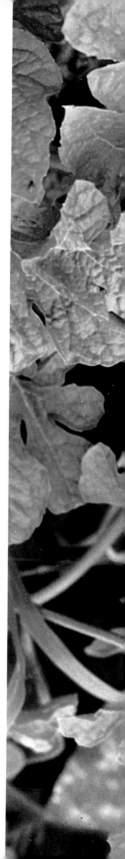

CHAPTER 5

BEING A GOOD DETECTIVE

In the first volume of *Gardening in the South,* I admonished you not to equate nature with our perfect God. In this chapter, you will see that nature in its fullness can be devastating. Believers in God have always pondered how the various plagues recorded over and over again fit into the scheme of our existence. Mankind has almost continuously faced myriads of attacks upon its plants. Insects have devoured its food, leaving starvation in their wake. Droughts and floods have dislocated millions and devastated their food supply; blights have wiped out huge numbers of people and sent their brothers to far-off lands.

When the first Japanese beetles arrived in the South, people were horrified to see droves of them devour roses or devastate grapes and plum trees. Nature can be cruel not only to the starving, but to each of us who have invested so much time and effort in our own gardens.

Fortunately we now have much more ability to ward off attacks like these. Perhaps our greatest technological breakthrough has been in the discovery of ways to lessen the impact of blights, insects, floods, and even droughts.

In the desert, young boys walk through freshly-sown grain fields beating upon large metal pans to prevent the flocks of birds from eating the new seed. The Egyptians have become quite adept at growing food, having learned thousands of years ago to lift water from the Nile and send it in canals for miles to keep the parched earth moist enough to support their crops. There are always problems when growing things. The problems may seem different in such diverse places as Egypt, Ethiopia, Palestine, Europe, the Philippines, and your garden, but they are similar in many ways.

IDENTIFYING THE PROBLEM

Solving a problem starts with its correct and positive identification. Sound silly? When you see thousands of Japanese beetles eating a plum tree, there is little doubt that to save the tree you must find a way to kill the beetles. Unfortunately, not all problems are that simple.

A leaf hopper

Japanese Beetles on roses in the Southern United States

A pencil point may cause the culprit to hop out.

White strands do not always mean a fungus is attacking. This is caused by a leaf hopper.

Look at the bottom of your plant for more definitive symptoms of the Blight disease.

Discoloration is a symptom of several different problems. On this tomato it is the beginning of a Blight attack.

Take a problem of hostas. The strands of white material seem to indicate that some sort of fungus is attacking these plants and the gardener should use a fungicide spray to control this attack. Look closer. You will see an insect hiding in this fungus-looking material. Meet the leafhopper! Controlling this attack takes an insecticide, not a fungicide. It is very easy to confuse the cause of one problem with the symptoms of another. Never jump to a conclusion. Be sure before you counterattack, for the wrong chemical will not produce the right results and can be harmful to the plant.

Tomatoes are very susceptible to blight. This disease may look like many other problems when it first invades the plant. Perhaps you have just been looking at your azaleas and have noticed a yellowing between the veins which indicates chlorosis due to an iron deficiency. The condition on your tomatoes may look like chlorosis when you first notice it. Observe further before you change the pH or spray with iron, which are the corrective measures for chlorosis. Farther down the plant may be more definite indications of blight. Notice the brown spots, the deterioration of the leaf edge, and perhaps the eventual drying-up of the bottom leaves. This is blight. You need a spray program with Maneb or some other recommended fungicide, not an application of iron or a soil treatment to change the pH. Solving problems is first and foremost a problem of true discovery. The gardener must be a good detective!

The first step toward finding a solution is observation and frequent inspection. The garden is a delightful place to stroll around, so take every opportunity you have to observe what is going on when you walk through it. I try to visit my garden every morning. This way I can see anything which might suddenly occur. The first attacks of blight might look like a lack of fertilizer, and so watch that plant for a day or two and see how the change is progressing. Soon you will know the exact cause of the problem. Sudden changes are the best clues with which to start being a good detective.

In our commercial vegetable projects we use a multi-check scouting system which includes observation by trained scouts, by the unit manager, by the production manager and by the farm manager himself. Even the

Know your plants and watch for changes. Our excellent Filipino scout, Gilbert, is charged with discovering problems before they become serious.

field workers are expected to report any changes which occur. We try to make everyone conscious of the need to find any problem which might suddenly show up instead of leaving the whole job to the technical staff and their trained scouts.

The plant itself is the focus of our inquiry. The entire plant growing in the garden is not visible. The top with its leaves, stems, and perhaps flowers and fruits are easily examined. Many times there seem to be no symptoms of disease or insect damage, and yet the plant may be off-color, weak, sometimes contorted, or with unusual growth, perhaps even dying. The unseen portion must now come under our scrutiny. Unfortunately a close examination of the root system might cause more damage to the plant from our inspection than from the action of the disease, insect, or growth problem. Here we need a lot of knowledge and a good bit of guessing. Plants with root diseases, insects, or the microscopic wireworm called a nematode have symptoms which give some clues.

Another serious problem has come with the advent of the growth regulator-type weed killers like 2-4-D. These materials are devastating to many types of plants. Drifting spray from lawn weed control can ruin trees, shrubs, and herbaceous flowers and vegetables. Tomatoes and dogwoods are extremely susceptible. The clues to this type of damage are easily recognizable. The foliage of affected plants becomes contorted, stems thicken and twist, and the plant has a strange appearance as if it were going through some grotesque growth cycle.

If we combine all of these, we can piece together a true picture. It takes observation, knowledge, and some guesswork to come up both with the cause of a problem and its best solution.

Discovery of root problems is difficult because you cannot see the affected part which is underground. The wilting of the plant is a sign to look at the roots.

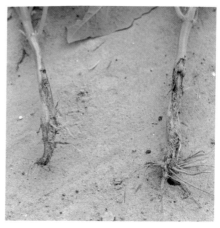

Digging of the bean plants shows a deteriorating root system with lesions on the lower stem which is a symptom of Fusarium root and stem disease.

Removal of this poorly growing and wilting tomato plant showed a Nematode attack on the roots.

Don't be hesitant to ask for help. Nurseries and garden centers, seed stores, plant outlets, many hardware stores, your local agricultural and forestry extension agents are happy to help solve your gardening problems.

All they, or I, can do is lead you to the answer by asking questions and offering possibilities. It is up to you to find the true answer.

TYPES OF PROBLEMS

There are many problems of great variations which occur. Finding what the problem is begins with the process of eliminating some of the various possibilities.

The laced leaves of this Brussels Sprout is easily identified as an insect attack.

Holes in a bean leaf indicate a Mexican Bean Beetle.

Even tiny holes like these on this eggplant leaf indicate an attack of Flea Beetles.

INSECTS

An insect attack is generally the easiest to discover when you can see the culprit. However, symptoms of insect attacks also give good clues. Laced leaves, mottled or off-color foliage, devoured leaves, stems cleanly cut at the ground, and holes in leaves, buds, flowers, and fruits are good indications that an insect is on the attack.

DISEASES

There are so many types of diseases around that discovery is generally a result of expecting something as much as seeing something. Since the pathogen is often a fungus whose strands are almost invisible, or a bacterium which can be seen only with a microscope, or a virus which is determined only by lab tests, recognizing the very specific symptoms of a disease is the best way to start a control program. There are many symptoms which indicate a disease attack. Dried-up stems of herbaceous plants, spots on stems and leaves, swollen leaves, discoloration, very regular holes in leaves, and sudden browning and dying of plant tips are some of the many symptoms of diseases which are common to the garden.

There are also times when the disease organism itself is evident. You can see the fungus when plants have mildew on the foliage or the fruits are covered with growing fungi which are plainly visible.

The bacterial disease, Fire Blight, on this pear must be identified from the symptoms of dead, hanging leaves.

Powdery Mildew on squash is identified by the visible fungus.

Dried spots on this cantaloupe leaf indicate an attack of an unseen fungus causing Downy Mildew disease.

A problem is discovered with these plums when they begin changing color before they are mature. Further observation finds the fungus itself on the fruit.

GROWTH OR PHYSIOLOGICAL PROBLEMS

This group of problems is the hardest to identify. Again, knowledge of what might occur and a careful analysis of the symptoms are the best ways to correct growth difficulties. Your plants may not have the color, growth rate, fruit set and development, flower size and number, or uniformity in the bed or row which they should. It is hard for those who lack experience with a given crop to know what is the norm and what is not. They must do a lot of guessing and ask for help from others with more experience.

In the Philippines where tropical humidity, high temperatures, and daily rain were different from my previous experience, I had to learn what to expect as if I were a first-year college horticulture student. Since we were growing crops which had never been tried in this area, there was little help from the local farmers. I had to take what these plants look like in other areas of the world and adapt my thinking to these new conditions.

The death of these beans was caused by poor drainage, which is indicated by algae on the surface.

Vegetables and fruits are particularly sensitive to nutrient deficiencies. These may include the lack of major or macro-nutrients as well as minor or micro-nutrients. The lack of a good fertilizer program which includes both classes of nutrients may cause severe problems for your plants.

Always use a *complete* fertilizer when growing vegetables, fruits, and herbaceous flowering plants. These include the major nutrients, nitrogen, phosphorus, and potash as well as the minor nutrients such as zinc, boron, magnesium, manganese, sulfur, copper, and iron.

Nutrient deficiencies are discovered by observing the growth of the plant. Nitrogen-starved plants are light in color; phosphorus-starved plants may have a purple cast as in the case of tomatoes and corn; while potassium-deficient plants grow poorly, have poor color, and often have brown edges to the leaves.

Nitrogen and potash are highly soluble in the forms used in fertilizers. Deficiencies may show up in years of very high rainfall while fertilizer programs may be adequate during years of low rainfall or even normal moisture. It is most important to be aware of the growth symptoms which indicate certain nutrient problems. Part of a gardener's scouting program must be to watch the growth of his plants for these nutrient effects.

Perhaps you have moved here from somewhere else and your plants look different and your results are not the same as before. From my Philippine experience, I understand what you are going through.

Yellowing of the leaves of these peanuts was quickly corrected by applying a nitrogen fertilizer.

The purple coloring of these corn leaves indicates a phosphorous deficiency.

Blossom End Rot of tomatoes is the result of a calcium deficiency.

The yellow to white streaks at the base of these corn leaves indicates a zinc deficiency.

FINDING THE ANSWER

The first step in this discovery process is to notice any change. The sheer enjoyment of being in the garden facilitates finding out what is wrong because we should be constantly looking at our plants. After all, that is why they are there—to look at and enjoy.

Much of this book is devoted to how you can grow plants better: choosing the right types, the right cultivars, and the right spot in the garden to plant; preparing the soil properly; growing the plant properly with the right fertilizers at the correct time; pruning at the right time; and solving problems which you might expect to have with outside agents such as too much rain, too little rain, or attacks from pests.

Investigation of the lower part of the tomato plant shows symptoms of Southern Blight, a deadly disease of the lower stem and roots. Note the white fungus growth right above the ground.

Further investigation shows symptoms of Blight.

This tomato plant is dying. The leaves have turned brown which might indicate a disease attack on the foliage.

The key to finding the answer to your plant's problem is to notice a difference and identify its cause. Plants will change subtly or drastically depending on the severity and cause of the problem. Damage from a deep, hard freeze may show up within a day or two after the freeze has passed. But an attack of spider mites may not become apparent for weeks or even months. The gardener must always be observant and use the process of elimination as well as identification to unravel the mystery of what is causing a plant to be less than it should be.

Plants are divided into parts: leaf, flower, trunk, stems and limbs, and roots. Each of these parts is subject to its own kind of problems. The leaves, flowers and structural part (stem or trunk and limbs) are easily observed, but the roots are out of sight and can be examined only with great difficulty, perhaps to the destruction of the plant. Root problems must be identified by the symptoms which they produce in the visible parts of the plant.

There is no way to list all the possible problems which might occur in your garden, nor define all the looks your plants might have. Much is in the eyes of the beholder. I have listened for many years on my call-in radio program to descriptions of plant problems and have heard the same symptoms described in many unique ways by different gardeners.

I offer the following as a guide to identifying your plants' problems, but I hope it will lead you to develop your own special identification techniques.

First, look closely at your plant.

1. Identify the obviously affected parts, such as discolored leaves.
2. Examine the whole plant further to determine if other areas have symptoms, like limbs which are shriveling.
3. Note the time of the year. Insects and diseases will be much less prevalent in winter than in summer. Cold damage will be seen only when the weather is freezing or soon thereafter.

TROUBLESHOOTING GUIDE

Although the focus of this volume of the series is on vegetables and fruits, your attention is seldom, if ever, confined to these plants alone. Most of us have many other plants in our gardens and landscapes which are just as susceptible to the problems which I am discussing.

Insects and diseases really do not care if the host plant is a fruit, a vegetable, a tree, shrub, or flowering plant. They will attack the host which they like. Sometimes, as in the case of spider mite attacks, they will move quickly from one class of plant to another. When the conditions are right for mildew on squash, they are also right for mildew on crepe myrtles although the pathogen is different.

The identification key which follows covers all types of plants and is designed for use whether the problem is first found on vegetables or flowers or some other favorite plant.

LEAF PROBLEMS

SYMPTOM	CAUSE	REMEDY
Leaves are off-color, light green, washed out; variegated leaves have lost some of the colors.	Plants may be in too much sun for the type.	Check the listings for exposure. Move plants to more shade or provide additional shade in that location.
	Plants may need more fertilizer, especially nitrogen fertilizer.	Check listings for proper fertilizer schedules.
	Plants may have root problems. a. Look at the total vigor of the plant. If you see weak, poor growth along with off-color,	Try to improve the drainage and work ground bark and perlite into the soil outside the root zone.
	b. Observe soil. Presence of algae or moss indicates poor drainage.	If this is the case, check listings for possible reactions to drainage problems.
Leaves are off-color and mottled or streaked, or veins stand out with a deeper color than the inter-vein area.		
Examine leaves for mottling (tiny spots).	Look on the underside of the leaf for residue or insects. Spider mites, scales, and lacebugs generally attack the underside.	Treat for specific insect infestation.
	Examine the top of the leaf. Many vegetable and herbaceous flower insects may be seen on the top side in the early morning or early evening.	Treat for specific insect infestation.

Examine leaves which have streaks for diseases as well as insects.

If the problem is worse at the bottom of the plant in the beginning, examine for fungus diseases.

Treat with a fungicide.

If the problem is at the top or on the sides in the beginning, it may be a virus disease.

Remove the plant from the garden.

If the problem is overall, it may be a growth problem, often caused by lack of micro-nutrients.

Use a fertilizer with micro-nutrients.

Examine leaves which have veins of deeper color than the area between the veins.

It may be chlorosis due to improper pH and a lack of iron in the soil.

Spray with an iron solution and acidify by using aluminum sulfate or an acid -orming fertilizer.

If found more prevalent at the bottom of the plant, especially in herbaceous plants, look for other leaves which have been affected for a longer time, since the problem may be a fungus. The older leaves may have developed blight symptoms.

Spray for blight.

Leaves have large spots.

This is often a fungus disease. It usually shows up as a nearly round infected area which spreads in all directions from the point of infection.

Treat with a fungicide.

Leaves have holes.

If the holes are irregular, it is usually caused by a chewing insect.

Treat for insect infestation.

If the holes are very regular, it is usually a shot-hole fungus.

Treat with a fungicide.

One winter this Liriope planting turned brown. Cold was found to be the cause by looking at the hardier English Ivy in the background which was also turning brown.

Mottling of these violet leaves indicates a problem.

The underside of the violet leaf shows definite indication of a spider-mite attack. These tiny insects are positively identified with a magnifying glass.

A geranium which needs nitrogen

Chewing insects make irregular holes as in the case of these Mexican Bean Beetles.

Worms have made these irregular holes in these corn leaves.

Large black spots on the green and yellow foliage of this rose are positive identification of Black Spot disease.

The yellow spots on these Boxwood leaves indicates an attack of Boxwood Leaf Miners, a serious insect pest.

This wilted squash showed no signs of a fungus attack but investigation showed a swollen lower stem. Cutting into the stem uncovered a Squash Vine Borer.

The soil is damp, yet these beans are wilting which indicates a severe root problem.

Pulling up a wilted plant shows root damage by a fungus.

Positive identification of these symptoms as a fungus attack results from a look at the whole plant and all the leaves to see the various stages of the disease.

LEAF PROBLEMS

SYMPTOM	CAUSE	REMEDY
Leaves are limp and wilting.	This may be caused by a lack of moisture. However, you should make further checks. Examine the soil to see if it is damp.	
	Wilting in damp soil indicates root problems.	Do not water; instead, check for poor drainage, root diseases or poor root development.
	Wilting in dry soil means extra water is needed.	Water properly.
	If neither is applicable, there may be stem or trunk problems. 1. In the case of herbaceous plants:	
	a. Check the base of the stem. If it is dry and shriveled, the cause may be a fungus or bacterial disease.	Check listings for proper fungicide or disease remedy. If diseased, remove plant from garden.
	b. Check for borers in the stem.	Treat for specific insect infestation.
	c. Wilting in herbaceous flowers and vegetables may be due to nematodes (microscopic wireworms) or root diseases. Dig up a representative plant and wash and inspect the roots.	
	1) Nematode infestations appear as knots on the roots or as club-like galls.	There is no remedy. Do not use this type plant in that area for three years.
	2) Root diseases generally appear as deteriorating roots, reduced root development, or dark brown rotten-looking roots.	Check listings for proper root disease treatment. Check for proper soil, water, and fertilizer.

Symptom	Possible Cause	Treatment

	2. In the case of woody plants, the cause may be damage to the trunk.
	  a. Check for borers in the bark.
	  b. Check for mechanical injury.
		Treat for borer infestation.

Edges of the leaves are brown.	1. Too much fertilizer
	2. Poor root development
	3. Over-watering
	4. Possible winter, stem, or root damage
	  a. Look at stems for bark damage.
	  b. Watch plant for poor new growth which would indicate root damage.
		Check listings to correct fault.

Leaves are brown during the winter.	This is usually cold damage or "burning." Roots are damaged by cold, or roots are inactive due to cold.	
Leaves are brown in the spring or summer.	Too much fertilizer Fire Blight on pears, apples, and crabapples	Check listings to correct. Follow a proper spraying schedule.
Leaves are dropping prematurely or abnormally.	Too little moisture Too much fertilizer Root diseases	Check listings to correct fault.
Leaves which are swollen	This is usually caused by a fungus.	Treat with a fungicide.
Leaves which are twisted, contorted, off-color, and misshapen.	May be caused by severe attacks of aphids and should be inspected for these insects.	Treat for aphid infestation.
	May be caused by hormone-type weedkiller spray or drift (2-4, D or similar type).	Correct use of these products. Let plant try to overcome the problem naturally.

Red spots on this poorly formed dogwood blossom indicate an infection of the fungus disease Dogwood Petal Blight.

No fruit followed this squash blossom. Examination showed it to be a male flower. Note the anther producing pollen.

FLOWER PROBLEMS

SYMPTOM	CAUSE	REMEDY
The entire blossom is shriveled after partially or fully opening.	Frost or freezing damage, especially when buds swell (camellias) during periods of extreme cold.	
	Fungus attacks (Botrytis on peonies, mildew on roses and crepe myrtles, blight on camellia and azalea cultivars).	Spray with a suitable fungicide.
Part of the flower is brown, usually the outer petals.	May be caused by thrips (tiny rod-shaped insects), aphids or other sucking insects.	Spray with a suitable insecticide.

Flower fails to open properly, being off-size or poorly developed.	May be caused by improper fertilizing or growth.	Check listings for proper fertilizer schedule.
	May be caused by insect damage.	Treat for specific insect infestation.
	May be caused by disease.	Remove plant from garden. Select disease-resistant varieties.
Flower fails to set fruit.	May be caused by improper pollination: a. No insects on transfer pollen b. No wind to transfer pollen (single rows of corn) c. May be a male flower (muscadines and squash-related plants) d. May be a female plant with no source of pollen (hollies and muscadines).	Correct pollination conditions.
	Plant may not be mature enough (tomatoes).	
	Plants may be growing too rapidly with too much nitrogen fertilizer.	Check listings for proper fertilizer schedules.
Flower drops very quickly.	May be the cultivar (check descriptions).	
	Soil may be too dry.	Water properly.
	May have too much nitrogen fertilizer.	Check listings for proper fertilizer schedules.

TRUNK, STEM, OR LIMB PROBLEMS

Sunken, shriveled bark on a pear tree is a good symptom of Fire Blight.

SYMPTOM	CAUSE	REMEDY
Bark broken or peeling.	Often caused by extreme cold (burst bark).	Cut below affected area and re-grow.
	Borers will loosen bark and cause it to peel.	Remove damaged tissue, clean wound and apply a wound dressing. Spray with a borer control material.
Bark removed cleanly.	When very near or slightly below the ground this may be caused by a mole or pine mouse which chews off the bark cleanly.	Keep mulch away from the trunk or lower limbs. Get a mean, hungry cat.
Stems or trunks which are weak or spindly.	The plants may be in too much shade.	Correct lighting conditions.
	The plants may have been given too much nitrogen or not enough phosphate or potash fertilizer.	Check listings for proper fertilizer schedules.
Stems of woody plants with sunken, shriveled bark.	In apples, pears, cherries and other plants of the same family (Rosaceae) it may be Fire Blight, a severe bacterial disease.	Prune each infected area 4 inches below the infection. Sprays are not effective. Plant Fire Blight-resistant cultivars.

FRUIT PROBLEMS

SYMPTOM	CAUSE	REMEDY
WOODY FRUITING TREES, SHRUBS AND VINES		
Small immature fruit falls as it begins to first increase in size.	The plant has been improperly pruned allowing more fruit to set than the tree can sustain.	Prune properly.
	The plants may have been given too much nitrogen fertilizer.	Fertilize properly.
	The plant may be suffering from drought.	Water properly.
	The young fruit may be attacked by a worm the egg of which was laid in the flower.	Spray with a suitable insecticide when tree is in flower.
Fruit falls as it begins to ripen.	The most common cause is the presence of a fruit worm. Examine the fruit and cut it open. If no worm is present or evidence is found that it was in the fruit, examine the skin.	Spray with a suitable insecticide when tree is in flower.
	Fruit rot will cause premature falling. Look for: a skin spot which has become soft and watery with decay, or strands of fungi on the skin.	Use lime-sulfur as a dormant spray. Spray with a fungicide as fruit begins to enlarge.
Fruit has jelly coming out but hangs on the tree.	This is the sign of a fruit worm.	Spray with a suitable insecticide when tree is in flower.
Fruit dries up while still on the plant.	Look inside: If hollow, it is the sign of a fruit worm.	Spray with a suitable insecticide when flower petals have fallen. Spray the ground around the plants.
	If the flesh is there but shriveled, it is generally a sign of drought.	Water properly.

FRUIT PROBLEMS

SYMPTOM	CAUSE	REMEDY
FRUIT PROBLEMS ON VEGETABLES		
Immature fruit drying up or falling off.	Improper pollination.	Correct pollination conditions.
	Too much or too little moisture.	Water properly.
	The plant is not mature enough or large enough to set the fruit.	
	Too much nitrogen fertilizer has been applied.	Fertilize properly.
Skips in kernels of corn.	Poor pollination.	Plant corn in blocks rather than single rows to give good pollination.
Yellow and white kernels of corn in the same ear.	Check variety. Some new varieties have both. Single color varieties which are planted too close to another color will have this problem.	
Tomato fruit are cracking.	Too much water followed by too little water or vice versa.	Water properly.
	Applying too much fertilizer when the fruit is maturing may cause this.	Fertilize properly.

Examine your plants' foliage and stems for sign of disease.

Tomato fruit are covered with skin blemishes or water spots.

Keep whole plant covered with Maneb spray.

These are caused by fruit worms.

Holes in fruits of tomato, pepper, eggplant, okra, and squash.

Control with Bacillus Thuringiensis, a biological insecticide.

The culprit is the cucumber pickle worm.

Holes in cucumber, honeydew, cantaloupe, and other melons on the underside of the developing fruit.

Dusting with Bacillus Thuringiensis is helpful but a simpler method is placing each fruit on a piece of plastic.

This is usually found on the first fruits when the plant is not mature enough to develop the fruit rapidly and during muggy weather.

Squash fruit are covered with a very visible fungus.

Removal is the best answer for spraying seldom helps.

Oversetting of many fruit trees will cause premature falling. Proper pruning and fertilizing will keep this from happening next year.

It is easy to find the worm causing the hole in this tomato. It is the Tomato Fruit Worm.

The Corn Ear Worm can devastate an ear of your best sweet corn.

The Black Fungus seen on this squash is seldom a problem after the plant is more mature and the fruits are developing rapidly.

Root problems are hard to identify since they are unseen.

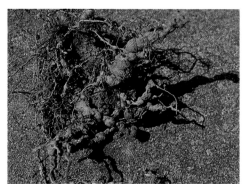

Nematodes can be disastrous, yet they are discovered only when the plant is dug and the soil removed.

ROOT PROBLEMS

The problems which occur in the root system of the plants are, perhaps, the most difficult to diagnose. You can't see what's happening! Root problems are therefore determined in three ways: (1) by the effect on the rest of the plant, (2) by what might be expected to happen, and (3) by taking a representative plant out of the ground, removing the soil, and inspecting the now-visible roots.

Throughout the guide are symptoms of root problems with the possible causes. Diagnose root problems by the symptoms seen in other parts of the plant whenever possible. The last resort is digging the plant for a detailed inspection, for by doing so you will destroy the plant in almost all cases.

NEMATODES

This terrible pest attacks an enormous number of plants including the tomato. Though there are a number of different nematodes, the one which is most commonly found on the tomato is the Root Knot Nematode. It is a pest of the root system which makes diagnosis difficult except by concentrating on its symptoms. Unfortunately, the symptoms are similar to those caused by a number of physiological as well as insect and disease problems. Any problem of the root system brings about certain changes in the plant's growth.

- Wilting
- Slower growth
- Poor color
- Browning of the leaf edges

Determining whether these symptoms are a result of nematodes, fungi, bacteria, insects or physiological problems is often impossible without digging up the plant and examining the roots.

There are three ways to prevent nematode problems:

- Grow nematode-resistant varieties
- Treat the soil with a nematocide prior to planting
- Plant tomatoes in a part of the garden where no tomatoes, peppers, eggplant, or okra have been grown for at least three years.

Modern hybridization gives us the best answer with the VFN hybrids. These are not only resistant to attacks by nematodes but are also resistant to the two major root diseases of tomatoes, Fusarium and Verticillium wilts.

I only plant varieties of tomatoes which are resistant to these problems. You will note that each of these varieties will have the letters VFN prominently attached to their names.

OVERCOMING PLANT PROBLEMS

After diagnosing a problem, the cure is often easy. At least it is easier to get information on a cure. The hardest part is proper identification of the symptoms but this is necessary to help your local garden dealer or County Extension Service advise you on the best chemical, fertilizer, or growing technique to use to overcome the problem.

Remember that fungicides have little, if any, effect on insects, nor does an insecticide have any chance of controlling a fungus attack. Herbi-

Guess what caused this problem. It was a rabbit eating the tender tops of these beans.

Here was a real stumper. What caused this splitting of a corn ear? Observation showed a crow did it.

cides (weed killers) can have disastrous effects on prized plants if applied in error. Proper diagnosis thus leads to the application of the best chemical or treatment for a plant's problem.

KNOWING WHAT CHEMICAL TO USE

You will note that I have given very few specific recommendations for controlling the above insects and diseases. New insecticides and fungicides are being introduced constantly. Old standbys may have been banned because of some problem which has been discovered. Each state has recommendations for its area.

I urge you to use the product which has been found to be best in your area. After identifying the problem seek the advise of your garden center, seed dealer, garden shop, hardware store or Extension Service as to the best materials to use.

The chart on page 221 should help you understand the terms used in the key.

SAFETY

Improper use of chemicals can be disastrous for plants. It can also be disastrous for you. Garden chemicals can be dangerous to your health if used improperly or haphazardly. **READ THE LABELS.** Follow all instructions and never use a chemical on a plant or plant type which is not listed on the label or in the brochure which accompanies the product. The following rules are most important.

1. Read the label.
2. Heed any cautions or warnings exactly.
3. Follow instructions for mixing the chemical.
4. Use only on plants listed on the label.
5. Observe any time restrictions prior to harvest.
6. **NEVER USE A CHEMICAL ON A FOOD CROP WHICH IS NOT SPECIFICALLY CLEARED FOR THAT PURPOSE.**
7. Mix only the amount needed for the current application. Never keep mixed chemicals on a shelf. When finished, dispose of the remaining mixed material.
8. Dispose of old chemicals. Never pour down a drain.
9. **KEEP CHEMICALS OUT OF THE REACH OF CHILDREN.**
10. Wear a long shirt, rubber gloves, goggles, and a respirator or filter over your mouth and nose.
11. Clean your sprayer thoroughly after each use.
12. Never use the same sprayer for herbicides which you use for insecticides and fungicides.
13. *Remember:*   **Diagnose Correctly**
   Use the Right Materials
   Protect Your Body When Spraying

PROBLEM		WHAT TYPE OF CHEMICAL TO USE
APHID	Insect	Insecticide
BACTERIAL WILT	Bacteria	None
BEETLE	Insect	Insecticide
BLIGHT	Fungus	Fungicide
BORER	Insect	Insecticide
BOTRYTIS	Fungus	Fungicide
CAMELLIA/AZALEA BLIGHT	Fungus	Fungicide
CHLOROSIS	Physiological	Iron Solution
FIRE BLIGHT	Bacteria	None
FRUIT ROT	Fungus	Fungicide
FRUIT WORM	Insect	Insecticide
FUSARIUM	Fungus	None
LACEBUG	Insect	Insecticide
LEAF GALL	Fungus	Fungicide
LEAF HOPPER	Insect	Insecticide
LEAF SPOT	Fungus	Fungicide
MILDEW	Fungus	Fungicide
MOSAIC	Viral	None
NEMATODE	Wireworm	Nematocide
PINE MOUSE	Rodent	None
SCALE	Insect	Insecticide
SHOT HOLE	Fungus	Fungicide
SPIDER MITE	Insect	Insecticide (Miticide)
THRIP	Insect	Insecticide
VERTICILLIUM	Fungus	None
VIRUS	Viral	None
VOLE	Rodent	None

Safety is a must when using chemicals. The Filipino on the left was well covered for spraying while the one on the right was protected while mixing. Note the long rubber gloves and the respirators.

GLOSSARY
COMMON VEGETABLE & FRUIT TERMS

AUBERGINE: The European name for eggplant.

BED: A raised planting area running the length of the row. A bed is generally made with an implement called a bedder which pulls soil from the middles and forms it into a long bed. The gardener can form a bed with a wing behind a tiller or with a hiller, or pull the soil from the middles with a hoe. A bed is used for root crops so that the bulbs, tubers, roots, etc. may form in loose soil.

BISEXUAL: Having both male and female parts in the same flower.

BLACK FROST: A frost which occurs when the temperature is below 32 degrees F. It is also called a killing frost because it destroys tender plants.

BLIGHT: A group of fungus diseases which is particularly devastating. Blight causes withering and dying without rotting.

BLOSSOM END: The end of the fruit to which the blossom is or was attached.

BORER: The larva of an insect which tunnels inside a plant part.

BOW RAKE: Also called a gardener's rake. This tool with heavy, sharp tines is useful for working soil lightly. It is contrasted with a spring tooth rake, also called a leaf rake, which is generally useless for working soil.

BROADCAST: To distribute seed or fertilizer in a broad pattern. Broadcasting may be done by hand or with an implement.

BULB: An underground storage organ for plants which is actually a modified leaf bud. It contains the bases of leaves which look like scales and which arise from a shortened fleshy stem.

BULBIL: A small bulb which may arise in some unusual place.

CALABRESE: The European name for broccoli.

CEREAL GRAIN: A field crop noted for the edible quality of the seed.

CHOKE: A common term used for the edible part of the artichoke.

COLD ENOUGH TO KILL A HOG: That time in the fall when the nights are cold and frosty and appropriate for slaughtering swine. The low temperature prevents spoiling of the meat while butchering. It is the time in the fall when tender plants are likely to be killed. It is also the time when I start itching to go to Egypt or some other warm place.

COLD FRAME: An unheated low structure partially buried and covered with a transparent or translucent material to trap the heat inside during the day and hold it during the night. Used for starting seeds in the winter and early spring and for rooting cuttings.

COLD GROUND: A phrase often used for garden soil which remains too cold for many seeds to germinate even though the danger of frost has passed. Most often the soil is cold and wet at the same time.

COOL OF THE EVENING: The time about dusk when the air is still and the temperature drops. It is a time of high fungus growth on plants. It is also a pleasant time in the garden after a hot day.

COTTON WEATHER: Hot, humid weather ideal for the growth of cotton.

COURGETTE: The European name for zucchini.

DAYS TO MATURITY: The number of days a vegetable takes to produce the first crop after the seeds have emerged. In a few cases it is the time noted which it takes to produce a crop after transplanting into the garden.

DETERMINATE: A term used to indicate certain plants, most often tomatoes, which have the same growth potential from the side branches as from the main shoot. When the side branches have formed and reach the length of the main stem, the side branches and the main stem grow at the same rate. Sometimes determinate plants are called self-topping plants.

DIOECIOUS: Male and female flowers are formed on separate plants. Vegetables are rarely dioecious.

DOG DAYS: Hot, sticky weather usually occurring from early July to late August. The term "dog days" is of Greek origin, so named because the hot, dry Greek summer generally began at the time Sirius, the dog star, rose with the sun. In Georgia, dog days are supposed to last for forty days. Tradition says that if it rains at the beginning of dog days, it will rain every day for forty days; if it is dry at the beginning of dog days, it will be dry for forty days.

DORMANT: The time when a plant is resting, usually during the winter when it is bare. Evergreens do not go into true dormancy but merely slow their growth to a minimum whereas a deciduous plant literally stops growing when dormant.

DRAINAGE: Movement of water through soil.

DRILL: The continuous planting of seed in a furrow with little regard for spacing.

DRIP IRRIGATION: Also called trickle irrigation. A method of irrigating plants by which water is pumped through small tubes. The tubes have tiny holes accurately spaced and have an internal flow design which gives equal pressure and water flow from end to end. The tubes are laid next to the plants or in some cases buried beside the rows or between them.

EAR: The seed-bearing organ of corn.

EQUINOX: The day in the spring and in the fall when the light hours equal the dark hours. The vernal equinox is that day in the spring (usually March 21) and the autumnal equinox is that day in the fall (usually September 22).

ESCULENT: Comes from the verb "to eat." An old term meaning something suitable for food.

FEEDING: A misnomer when applied to fertilizing plants. Plants produce their own food from photosynthesis, but must have the macro- and micro-nutrients or major and minor elements for growth, flower, and fruit. The correct way to describe the application of nutrients is to say "fertilizing plants" not "feeding plants."

FERTILIZATION: The union of the male and female gametes to form a fertilized cell or zygote which becomes the seed. The term is mis-applied when used to mean applying fertilizer.

FERTILIZING: Applying fertilizer.

FROSTY MORN: The early light hours when one awakes to find the garden covered with frost. A time to move farther south.

FURROW: The trench made in well-prepared soil into which seed or plants are placed. A furrow may be made in flat ground or in a bed.

FURROW IRRIGATION: Method of applying water to a garden area by running the water on the ground, usually in the middles, so that it slowly enters the furrow.

FURROW SLICE: The depth of tillage or plowing of a field or garden.

FURROWER: An implement used to make a furrow.

GONE TO VINE: Vegetative growth at the expense of fruiting or flowering growth.

GOOSENECK HOE: A modern hoe which has a steel rod from the flat part of the hoe to the metal socket which holds the handle.

GRASS: The English term for asparagus.

GREEN MANURE: Herbaceous plant material which is turned under the ground to build the soil. Often, but not exclusively, a legume like Crimson Clover and Austrian Winter Peas.

GREENS: The common term for vegetables whose green parts are boiled and eaten (with great delight, I must add).

GUMBO: The Louisiana name for okra.

HALF-RUNNER: A type of bean which has short tendrils but which, unlike bush beans, must have some support.

HARD FREEZE: Temperatures low enough for the cells of tender plants to form ice, which kills them. The temperature is usually below 28 degrees F.

HARDPAN: The hard layer of farm or garden land which lies beneath the furrow slice and which has little growth potential.

HARVEST MOON: The full moon of late October or early November which coincides with hard frost and the final harvest of the season.

HILL: A raised mound in and over a furrow which allows seed to germinate in dryer soil than is found in the furrow, where water tends to stand in the spring.

HILLER: A winged implement used to push soil from the middle to the side to make a bed.

HOT BED: A cold frame which has an electric heating cable in the soil to keep seed warm as they germinate. It can refer to any tray or planting area with a buried heating cable.

IMMUNE: Not susceptible to a disease or insect.

INDETERMINATE: The type of growth on certain vegetables, mainly tomatoes, where the main stem continues to grow at a faster and stronger rate than the lateral growth off the main stem. In tomatoes, it indicates a longer bearing season.

INORGANICS: In gardening this specifically applies to fertilizers which are not produced by animals or plants. The macro-nutrients nitrogen, phosphorus, and potash are industrially manufactured in a form which is most usable to most plants. Generally, but not always, bacteria do not have to act on these nutrients to render them usable for uptake into the plant by the roots.

INSIDE BUD: A growth bud which lies on the side of the branch facing toward the leader or center of the plant.

KILLING FROST: A frost so heavy that it kills tender plants.

LATERAL BUD: A growth bud which is on the side of a branch or stem.

LAY BY: An old farming term meaning the time of the last cultivation of corn or cotton and usually accompanied by the last fertilizer application. From laying by until harvest, the plants are on their own.

LEADER: The name given the prominent central trunk of any tree. The terminal bud of the leader takes growth precedence over all other buds.

LEGUME: A specific family of plants which attracts nitrogen-forming bacteria to the root system. These bacteria live in nodules on the roots and take nitrogen from the air, converting it into the nitrate form which is readily taken into the roots of plants. Beans, peas, clovers, and the alfalfas are common legumes.

LIME: In gardening, it generally refers to ground limestone rock which is a slow-acting form of calcium, added to the soil to raise the pH.

LONG DAYS: The days between the spring equinox and the fall equinox when the number of light hours is greater than the number of dark hours.

MACRO-NUTRIENTS: The major plant nutrients: nitrogen, phosphorus, and potash. The symbols N, P, and K refer to these nutrients.

MESS: As in a mess of beans. A good Southern expression all new gardeners should adopt. It means a gathering, usually for a meal.

MICRO-NUTRIENTS: Minor or trace elements needed by most plants for healthy growth. Most soils have a supply of most of these, but it is helpful to add them at least once a year in most instances.

MIDDLE: The area between two furrows.

MIDDLE-BUSTER: An implement used to work the middle, usually fairly deeply.

MILDEW: A white or gray-beaded fungus.

MINOR ELEMENTS: The same as micro-nutrients.

MOISTURE HAS MET: When the subsoil moisture and the surface moisture meets in the furrow slice, allowing complete capillary action to take place.

MONOECIOUS: Flowers of separate sexes on the same plant.

N,P,K: Chemical symbols for the macro-nutrients nitrogen, phosphorus, and potash.

NEMATODES: Microscopic wireworms which attack and destroy the roots of susceptible plants.

NETTED: The term applied to the pattern occurring on certain cucurbita species which Americans call cantaloupes or muskmelons.

OPEN GROUND: Areas free from shade.

ORGANICS: Materials which come from animals or plants and thus have carbon compounds as their basis.

OUTSIDE BUD: A growth bud which lies on the side of a branch facing away from the leader or center of the plant.

OVERHEAD IRRIGATION: Sprinkler watering where the implement sends the water up and out to fall on the plants from above.

PASCHAL MOON: The spring moon nearest to Easter and the vernal equinox.

PERFECT: In horticulture, this refers to flowers with both male and female parts within the same blossom.

pH: A scale or rating of the acidity and alkalinity of the soil.

PIMENTE: The Spanish name for pepper.

PLOW: Using an implement to break up the soil. A plow is a metal implement which is pulled through the soil to break it up and on occasion to move it.

PLOWING TO: Using a plow to move soil, after breaking it up, toward a bed or toward plants.

POLLINATION: The transfer of the pollen from the male part to the female, causing fertilization.

POMME DE TERRE: The French name for the Irish potato.

POST-EMERGENCE: After the plants are up.

POST-HARVEST: After harvest, specifically the handling of vegetables after harvest.

POTATO: The name applied primarily to an edible underground root or tuber, as sweet potato or Irish potato. Country people have traditionally referred to many underground storage roots as potatoes, like 'dahlia potatoes.'

POTATO HOOK: A hand-implement with tines used to dig potatoes.

PRE-EMERGENCE: Prior to the germination of seed.

PRE-HARVEST: Before the harvest.

PRE-PLANT: Before planting.

RESISTANT: Plants which are not adversely affected by a disease or insect, though either might be present.

RHYZOME: A stem at or below the ground level which has the ability to send up shoots.

RIDGE: Another name for a bed.

ROOT ZONE: The soil area which is inhabited by the roots of a plant.

RUNNING: A viney plant, usually but not always with tendrils.

SCRAPE: A type of plow which is used to scrape the ground and cut the weeds which have formed.

SEEDLING: A small plant grown from a seed.

SETTING: Putting plants in the ground, as setting out tomatoes.

SHORT DAYS: The days between the fall equinox and the spring equinox when the number of dark hours is greater than the number of light hours.

SIDE-DRESSING: Applying fertilizer in a band beside a row of growing plants without getting any on the foliage or stems. In the field, side-dressing is done with an implement which places the fertilizer in the ground and covers it. In the garden, the fertilizer is applied by hand and worked into the soil with a hand cultivator. Side-dressing is done during the growing season whenever fertilizer is needed.

SILK: The female receptacle on corn onto which the pollen falls to fertilize the kernels in the ear.

SLIPS: Small plants, usually sweet potatoes, grown from the previous crop's potatoes.

SOAKING: Wetting thoroughly.

SPRINKLING: Watering lightly.

SPROUTS: Usually, but not always, refers to side shoots of vegetables.

STEM END: The end of the fruit to which the stem is attached.

STICKY SOIL: Wet, heavy clay soil which you cannot work well.

STRINGING: Tying viney or running plants to a support.

SUB-SOIL: The soil area below the furrow slice which is usually of such poor quality that plants grow poorly.

SUCKER: In vegetable gardening, the tomato shoot which arises between a leaf and the stem.

TASSEL: The male, pollen-bearing part of corn which arises at the terminal of the plant.

TERMINAL BUD: A growth bud which is at the tip of a branch or stem. The terminal bud of the leader takes precedence over all other buds.

TERRACE: In the field or garden, a level area which has been formed on a slope.

TILLER: A power implement with rotating tines which pulverize the soil.

TOO WET TO PLOW: A condition occurring when the soil is so wet that working it will ruin the structure.

TRANSPLANTING: Taking a small plant from the place where it was started and planting in a pot or directly in the garden.

TUBER: A storage organ formed at the end of a rhyzome which has the parts of a stem in modified form.

TURN THE GARDEN: Taking soil from underneath the ground and placing it on top of the ground, i.e., reversing the soil's position with an implement.

VEGETABLE MARROW: The European name for winter squash.

WANE OF MOON: The time from the full moon to a new moon.

WARREN HOE: A sharp, pointed hoe which is used for making furrows easily.

WATER FURROW: The wetness in a furrow found in periods of great rain.

WAX OF MOON: The time from the new moon to the full moon.

WET TO DRIP: Spraying a plant until the time when the spray is great enough that it begins to drip off the plant.

WING PLOW: A plow with a side metal piece shaped like a wing used to cut off weeds at the ground and to move soil toward the plants in the row. Similar to a scrape.

WOOD ASH: Country name for ashes which contain high phosphate.

INDEX